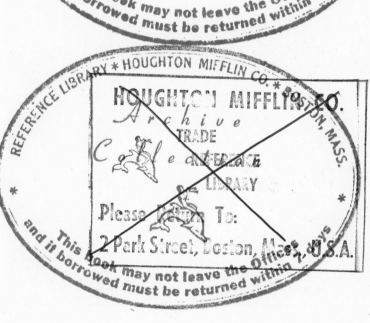

CRAZY HORSE

CRAZY HORSE

Great Warrior of the Sioux

by

SHANNON GARST

Illustrated by
WILLIAM MOYERS

Houghton Mifflin Company · Boston

To
My Son
WARREN

CONTENTS

CRAZY HORSE

BATTLE
WITH
THE
WASPS

■■■■■■■ 1

AN AIR OF TENSENESS and foreboding hung over the camp of the Oglala Sioux all of that strange summer. First came the terrifying time when an ominous black shadow moved across the sun, making the world dark in the middle of the day. Women and children screamed. Warriors rushed from their tepees and fired arrows at the shadow until it finally let the sun come again.

Everyone knew that such a fearsome event must be a forewarning of disaster or danger.

Has-ka's father was a holy man in whose lodge important things were often discussed. Therefore Has-ka was more aware than most boys of the uneasiness among his people — of the feeling that gigantic events were in the making.

It all had to do with a race of men with white skins and with something they called the "Gold Rush." Has-ka did not know what the words meant, but because he asked questions about everything, he asked about this.

1

"Gold," his father explained as he skinned a deer for the stew pot, "is shining, yellow dirt which drives white men crazy. Far off toward the setting sun is a place where this shining dirt is found. That is why the palefaces are crossing our land, frightening away the game and the buffalo herds."

"But the white men go on. They do not stay." Has-ka squatted down to watch his father's skillful hands at work.

"No. They do not stay — yet," agreed his father. "They pass quickly and do not return."

"Then let them pass along their trail," Has-ka shrugged. "Our plains are wide. The herds go to the hills. I like it best when our camps are in the mountains."

His father shook his head. "You are but a boy," he said. "It is hard for you to understand how evil descends upon our people whenever the white man comes. Already the Blue Coats have taken over the place called Fort Laramie — a place once held as a trading post by our trapper friends. It is not good."

"I have never seen the place called Laramie. I have never seen a Blue Coat," Has-ka broke in.

"It would be better if you did not see them — ever," his father told him.

Has-ka's mind did not dwell upon his father's words. Those were things about which the old men talked and which seemed to have little to do with him just then. He had more immediate and personal concerns and one especially which right now seemed to him to overshadow everything else. He had discovered only recently that he was different in appearance from other Indian boys, being fairer in coloring. He was called Has-ka, meaning light-skinned one. His hair, too, was not like that of other Indian boys, but was brown and rather wavy.

At first he did not think about the matter too much — until something occurred which drew his attention entirely to himself and made him feel tragically set apart.

It was soon after his father had explained to him about the Gold Rush and the coming of the soldiers to Fort Laramie that it happened. He was squatted by the stew pot one day, dipping into it with a big horn spoon when No Water, grandson of Chief Smoke, ran through the village yelling, "I have discovered a wasp nest! Come all of you warriors. We will give battle to the enemy. Drive him from our land."

Has-ka leaped to his feet. A favorite game of Indian boys was to make war on bees or wasps, pretending they were fierce foes — an exciting sport not without painful dangers. Indian boys came running from every direction. They dashed into their tepees to daub themselves with war paint, then scampered after No Water.

Has-ka, too, hurriedly dipped fingers into the paint pots his father used to decorate ceremonial drums, daubing his face with their colors, wishing as he did so that his father were a warrior with a special bag of war paints. Grabbing his bow and blunt arrows, he dashed off to join the band of howling young savages on their way to do battle with the wasps.

Coming close to the "enemy" No Water put his finger to his lips as a signal for silence. The boys crept quietly through the brush and grass. Has-ka, the youngest of the group, tagged light-footedly along behind them.

Then with wild war whoops the young redskins, led by No Water, dashed toward the tree in which the wasp nest hung. They struck the nest with sticks, knocking it to the ground. Has-ka yelled with all his might but he was not strong enough to force his way through the group to the nest. He had to wait until it had been kicked about and its inhabitants thoroughly aroused. As his comrades scattered he ran to the nest and jumped on it, yelling, "I, the brave Has-ka, do today by myself kill the fierce enemy."

The words were scarcely out of his mouth before the wasps attacked him. His yells of triumph turned to screams of pain.

"Run to the river," He Dog cried.

Has-ka raced for the stream and dived in. When he came out, his face and body were red and lumpy from many wasp stings. Ignoring the burning pain he ran to join in the victory dance about the trampled wasp nest but his comrades shoved him out of the circle.

"You disgraced the Oglala tribe," No Water told him, his voice hoarse with contempt. "You cried out when the wasps stung you. You are a girl! No Sioux brave cries out from pain."

Disgraced and scorned, Has-ka sat on a log to watch the others in their victory dance. When it was over, the boys went back to the village, jabbering loudly of their coups. They did not even glance at Has-ka, sitting so forlorn and miserable upon the log.

After their laughing chatter had died away in the distance, an immense silence fell upon the forest, and with it a chill upon Has-ka's spirits.

How could he face his comrades again, he wondered. They would never forget the disgraceful thing he had done. How could he ever hold up his head among them?

He got to his feet and walked slowly to the near-by stream where there was a quiet, peaceful pool. He slid to his stomach to peer into its depths to see if any trout swam below. Then a shadow of dissatisfaction crossed his face. The still water gave back to him his own reflection — the fair skin

and hair which set him apart from other Indians and which had won for him the detested name of Has-ka — light-complexioned one.

Why was he not dark like other Sioux boys? That he had the high cheek bones, the straight nose and steady black eyes which were the Sioux standard of handsomeness meant nothing to him. He was conscious only that his skin was the dull tan of a ripe acorn instead of coppery, and that his hair was nearly as fair as his skin and, most hateful of all — it had a slight wave, like his sister's when she loosened her braids.

"Ugh!" he grunted in disgust, shoving himself to his feet and picking up his bow and arrow. He stood slim, straight and naked save for his breechclout and moccasins. He glared at the full-length reflection, then stooped and picked up a rock flinging it into the pool with all his might shattering his image. He turned and strode through the woods toward the camp, his angry thoughts buzzing around in his head like a swarm of aroused bees.

If only he were like other Indian boys. If only he could be one who stood out as a leader and have a manlike name instead of the detested Has-ka! If only he were one whom the old men mentioned about the campfires as a boy of great promise — as No Water was.

Thinking of him, Has-ka felt a twinge of envy. No Water, a stalwart boy about two snows older than he, was the sort of Oglala he wished he could be — always a leader, sure of himself, admired and envied by all the boys of the village, and one who had even attracted the notice of the older men. No feast had ever been held in Has-ka's honor. Most of the time he moved through the camp unnoticed by anyone except for two or three grateful old men who re-membered that during the cold winter, when he was only four snows old and people were starving, he had, without consulting the family, invited the hungry ones to his tepee to partake of the two elk his father had brought in. His family later went hungry because of his generosity, but for a time people had smiled at him and patted his head when he went by.

In this black mood he was dissatisfied even with his family. Why did Crazy Horse, his father, and also his grandfather, have to be holy men of the tribe? Why had his father not been a warrior or a chief, so that he, Has-ka, would as a matter of course be looked up to and be chosen a leader of games? Because he was clumsy of tongue he was known as "the silent one." Although he was nine snows old, he had never been chosen leader of anything. He blamed his lack of importance on the fact that his father was a holy man instead of a chief. Never had he blamed his set-apartness on himself.

The boughs of the trees strained the sunlight, making patches of golden light on the ground. Has-ka moved swiftly, but as silently as a breeze, his observant eyes taking in every tiny footprint, every turned leaf or grass blade, every sign on the forest floor. He decided that nothing of any size had moved here recently; the woods seemed deserted of life. He was disappointed for he had hoped to find some sort of game to take back to camp so that his people would notice him, and forget the disgrace of his conduct during the battle with the wasps.

He wished that something would happen so that he could prove his bravery — give him a coup to tell of beside the campfire. Well he knew that counting coup — striking an enemy a telling blow with the bare hand or a special, decorated stick, was the thing for which every Sioux warrior strove.

As he walked along the silent, woodland path he even imagined himself battling a band of Crow Indians — saving his own tribe from destruction. But when he came from the thinning forest to the Oglala village where the painted tepees of his tribe stood in a circle beside the river, his brief feeling of triumph over his imaginary battle evaporated. Old men dozed in the shade against their backboards. Naked children romped in the grass. Women bent over the hides they were scraping, or sat beside the tepees sewing dyed porcupine quills onto moccasins or decorating their own white deerskin robes with them. Their papooses slept in their cattail-lined cradle boards suspended from pliable tree limbs which swayed in the breeze. A handful of older boys galloped their horses up the river flat. Another group shouted and splashed in the river. They paid no attention to Has-ka as he slipped by them without greeting.

The Oglala Sioux were camped in a pleasant valley protected by the Black Hills. It was a quiet, peaceful spot and the Crow tribe Has-ka had pretended to battle was far away. Again he was a lonely, unimportant boy.

As he came near his own tepee, he saw his stepmother, Gathers-Her-Berries, seated on the ground sewing dyed porcupine quills onto a deerskin dress for his sister. She was like a bird, he thought, with her quick, quiet movements, and the dark, smooth hair lying back on her head was like raven wings. He could not remember his own mother.

His stepmother smiled and rose to her feet when she saw him. "I have buffalo meat in the pot," she said. "I will make it warm for you."

With a forked stick she lifted hot rocks from the fire just outside the entrance to the tepee and dropped them into the buffalo-paunch pot which hung on a pole rack over the coals. The water bubbled, releasing savory odors of buffalo

meat flavored with wild onions and turnips. Has-ka's mouth watered. He stepped into the tepee and brought out a spoon made from a buffalo horn, which he dipped into the stew. First, offering the mixture to the sky, the earth and the four directions, he picked out chunks of tender meat and stuffed them into his mouth.

His father came from the lodge where a meeting of councilors of the tribe was being held. He was a short, slim man with quiet, understanding eyes. His eyes smiled now as he saw his older son.

"How is it with you, my boy?" he asked.

"It is well with me, my father," Has-ka replied. Evidently his family had not heard of his disgrace or his parents would not have looked at him with such kindness and fondness.

He saw his little sister, Laughing One, with a group of girls playing with their wooden dolls. He saw his younger brother, Little Hawk, splashing in the stream with other noisy boys. With the warm food in his stomach and the quiet affection of his family surrounding him, he forgot his unhappiness. He was at least important in his own family and for the present that was enough.

FIRST

COUP

2

T HE MORNING AFTER the battle of the wasps, Has-ka slept later than usual. He rose and ran to the stream to wash before he faced the sun in morning prayers.

His father, Crazy Horse, was sitting cross-legged outside the tepee, painting a zigzag lightning design on a ceremonial drum of rawhide stretched over a piece of a hollow log which was partly filled with water. His paints, made of powdered berries or colored earth, were in small turtle shells. First he sketched on the ground the design he wanted to follow, then using the frayed end of a bone he applied his paints to the drumhead.

Has-ka sat on the ground to watch, fascinated by his father's slow, rhythmic motions. Always he was like this — deliberate about everything he did, as though there were no need for hurry about anything. Always there was an air of serenity and strength about him. It gave the boy a feel-

'ing of comfort to watch those slow movements of his father's hands — so different from his stepmother's darting, birdlike motions.

"You are quiet today," his father said, noticing his son's sober expression. "Why are you not with the other boys in their games?"

"I have no wish for games," he said briefly.

His father gave him a quiet, questioning look, but said nothing more. Has-ka could not tell his father why he shrank from joining his comrades — that his deepest desire was to avoid them.

For several days he stayed apart from them, until he almost forgot the wasp episode. But he was not allowed to forget it very long.

The first time he joined his playmates after his disgrace, No Water chanted, "Here comes the girl — the light-haired one who cries when the wasps sting."

The others took up the chorus. Has-ka held his head high and made his face a mask so that his tormentors could not see how their taunts stung.

"I will show them!" he secretly vowed. "I will be braver than the bravest. Someday, I, Has-ka, will be great among all of the Seven Council fires of the Sioux."

Whenever his friends taunted him, he silently made this vow. It gave him a sense of power and the strength to endure the ridicule of his comrades without showing emotion.

Gradually, though, other concerns drew the attention of the boys. Their memories of the wasp battle dulled and it was mentioned less and less frequently, and finally was apparently forgotten.

After the passing of another snow, the edge of Has-ka's shame became dulled for him, too, and he seldom remembered the affair. Now something was to happen which was to make a great difference in his life.

One day his father said in his quiet way, "It is time you had your own horse, my son."

Has-ka sucked in his breath. For many moons he had longed for a horse which belonged to him alone.

"To make an animal really yours," his father went on, "you must break him — train him yourself."

"*Hau!*" Has-ka said eagerly. "That is what I want to do."

"Come with me then." His father led the way to a sprawling pole corral behind the camp.

The boy knew that his father was not rich in the way the Sioux measured wealth — in the possession of many ponies. He had only a few which had been given him by Oglalas whom he had counseled wisely. Being a holy man he did not make a practice of stealing horses from enemy tribes — the occupation which was the main sport of the Sioux.

"Choose," the holy man said when they came to the corral.

The boy's eyes gleamed as he looked the animals over. His glance kept returning to a fine-bodied raven black stallion cropping grass at the far end of the corral.

"That one," he said, pointing.

"The others are less wild," his father said. "Some of them have been ridden."

A surge of disappointment swept over Has-ka. Already he had pictured himself riding this fine animal.

"That one," he insisted stubbornly, pointing again.

His father shrugged and Has-ka thought that he looked pleased. *"Was-te!* Good!" He smiled. "You have chosen wisely. It will be the best pony of them all if you train him well. Commence now." He pointed to a long stick to which was tied a horsehair rope with a slip loop at the end.

Has-ka's eyes gleamed with excitement as he entered the corral, taking a headstall from a pole and holding the noose in one hand. He knew what to do. Many times he had watched warriors break and train their ponies.

His hands were trembling as he slipped the headstall on the strong brown horse his father often rode. Grasping the mane, he vaulted to the horse's back and rode toward the pony he had chosen.

The stallion's well-shaped head came up, the ears perked forward, the eyes held alarm.

"Quiet, *kola,* my friend." Has-ka's voice was soothing. "You are mine. We will be friends. I will not harm you; I will care for you. We will hunt the buffalo together; steal ponies from the Crows. You shall carry me far and I will call you Strongheart."

While he was speaking he edged close, slowly thrusting the loop out. The black horse sniffed the noose, then wild-eyed, snorted and raced to the other side of the corral.

Slowly Has-ka rode toward him again, talking soothingly, pushing out his loop. Time and again his noose almost settled over the black head. Then with a snort or a whinny the pony was away.

Has-ka's patience began to wear thin. "You are teasing me, my friend," he cried. "Let us get this thing finished."

His father had long ago grown weary of watching the performance in the corral and had gone back to his tepee. The sun had started its downward path toward the edge of the world before Has-ka finally succeeded in settling the noose over Strongheart's head.

A whinny like a shrieked challenge came from the throat of the splendid animal at this indignity. He lunged from side to side, reared and pawed the air, but with Has-ka's strong mount holding him, with the loose end of the rope around its neck, the slip knot of the noose slowly choked the breath from the struggling Strongheart.

"Do not fight, my friend!" the boy begged. "I have no wish to choke you — but that is what I must do . . . "

It seemed to Has-ka that the black horse would never cease struggling, but with his lungs denied air by the cruel rope, he was finally forced to cease fighting. His head drooped between his forelegs.

Quickly Has-ka leaned forward to loosen the noose, rubbing the sweaty neck as he did so. With great, panting breaths Strongheart drew precious air back into his lungs, then the struggle resumed — but not so hard or so long this time.

The boy was so exhausted his knees nearly buckled beneath him when he at last dismounted, but he was pleased, for Strongheart had learned that it was useless to struggle against the rope around his neck. He was an intelligent horse; training him would not be too difficult.

Twice a day Has-ka went to the corral, roped Strongheart and worked with him, later throwing a blanket on his back, then pulling it off time and again to get him used to the feel of weight. Every day he carried sweet grass from the edge of the creek and gave a whistle signal which Strongheart at last learned to obey.

Then came the day to which Has-ka had been looking forward — yet dreading. He led Strongheart to a stump from which he eased himself onto his back. In spite of the long gentling process, the black horse bucked all over the corral, twice hurtling Has-ka to the ground. Bruised and angry, he picked himself up and tried again until finally he managed to stay on. Then with knees, hands and voice he guided Strongheart around the corral. Day after day this training went on until the black horse allowed the boy to ride any time he chose.

After he had ridden him the first time without a struggle, Has-ka stood looking at him triumphantly. "You are mine!" he cried.

Something happened to his spirit then. He had mastered a creature far stronger than he. There was power in him. Power to master animals. At the moment he felt that nothing was impossible for him to accomplish.

Grasping the black mane, he again vaulted to Strongheart's back and rode out of the corral and through the village with head high, eyes ahead, hoping that the other boys would notice him on this splendid horse. Now he had a friend who would never taunt him for his light skin or the affair with the wasps.

Before long he was acknowledged to be one of the best riders in the village — a prominence which was very pleasant to his bruised self-esteem. He shoved all thought of his recent disgrace into the depths of his mind. Not yet

was he a leader among the Oglala boys, but neither was he the lowliest among them. And some day he would be great!

Another snow had come and gone and again it was the moon of berries ripening.

One morning his father said, "You will bring in the pony herd. In my dreams last night I saw the Crows drive off many of our horses."

Has-ka dipped into the steaming stew pot for his breakfast. His father was a prophet. His dreams often foretold things that would happen. The boy's heart beat faster at the prospect of some excitement if the Crows did try to steal their ponies.

"Come with me, younger brother," Has-ka said to Little Hawk. "We will ride my fine horse, Strongheart."

Little Hawk's eyes sparkled. To him at least Has-ka was a hero and he liked nothing better than to tag along after him, doing the things he did, or at least giving a fair imitation.

"I wish our father would give me a pony of my own," Little Hawk said, following his older brother into the tepee.

"He will do so," Has-ka said soberly, "as soon as you are old enough to tame your pony yourself — as I did Strongheart."

Has-ka picked up his quiver of arrows and threw it over his shoulder. His bow that he had made of willow was still in his hand. He reached up for his hair rope which hung on a tepee pole, it was often a handy thing to have along.

The two boys walked to the pole corral. Has-ka gave a shrill whistle and Strongheart pricked up his ears, whinnied and trotted toward him.

Has-ka slipped the headstall on and looped the hair rope loosely over the stallion's neck, then took hold of the black mane with one hand and vaulted onto the horse's back.

Reaching down, he grasped Little Hawk's hand and pulled him up behind him.

Has-ka pounded his moccasined heels against Strong-heart's sides. This morning as the horse broke into a lope and the soft air brushed his cheeks, he experienced the wild feeling of importance and elation he always felt when riding. He rode without saddle, pressing with his knees against the pony's sides to guide him. Whenever he rode, it felt as if he and his mount were a part of each other. His body swung to the rhythm of the hoofbeats and the animal appeared to sense his wishes, as though one mind guided them both.

On their way to the grassy plains where the pony herd usually grazed, they passed a thicket where raspberries hung thick and tempting.

"*Hopa!*" Has-ka cried, stopping his horse with a pull on the mane. "Fill your belly with green grass, Strongheart, while we fill ours with berries." He left his rope across the horse's neck and he slipped his arm through his bow so that he could use both hands to pick the fruit.

As the boys stuffed handfuls of berries into their mouths, it became a race to see which could pick and eat the faster, each laughing loudly at the funny sight the other made with berry juice smeared from ear to ear.

But suddenly their laughter froze in their throats, for as they raced along picking the largest, ripest berries, the thicket ended abruptly in a clearing where a mother grizzly bear with two cubs had been asleep in the warm grass. With a startled roar the great animal sprang to her feet with a speed which belied her clumsy appearance. Her eyes were red-rimmed, her enormous teeth bared. Quickly she started toward them.

Little Hawk stood as if paralyzed, and for a long moment Has-ka's mind and muscles were as if paralyzed, too.

"H-Has-ka!" Little Hawk's voice quavered on a thin note of terror.

The great bear was lunging closer. At the sound of his brother's cry, Has-ka's brain and muscles responded — his own fear forgotten. With a strength he hadn't known he possessed he seized Little Hawk and shoved him up into the crotch of a small tree. Then giving his shrill whistle he raced through an opening in the thicket toward his horse with the bear so close that he imagined he could feel her hot breath on his bare back.

Strongheart came trotting to the edge of the thicket in response to his master's signal. The pony had not seen the great bear, but as Has-ka popped from the bushes, the horse caught sight of the charging grizzly and the boy had just time to seize Strongheart's mane and leap to his back before the horse, with a snort of terror, was away like an arrow from a bow. At first Has-ka was glad to be on Strongheart's back racing away from the grizzly; then fear for his brother's welfare overcame his concern for his own safety. He tried to guide the terrified pony back toward the clearing in the thicket, but his efforts failed. He realized that he would have no control over the rushing horse until Strongheart had run off the fear of the bear, so he urged the horse to greater and greater speed all the while guiding him in a large circle toward the tree in which he had left Little Hawk.

In time the horse lost his great burst of speed and gradually slowed down, soothed by Has-ka's words, "Quiet, my friend, quiet." The boy finally maneuvered the winded horse through the thicket into the opening near where Little Hawk still clung to his dangerous perch. The bear was stretching greedy claws up the tree which was little more than a sapling.

Has-ka beat Strongheart with the rope and pounded him
with his heels in an effort to get the horse to charge the
bear but again Strongheart bolted.

Has-ka knew he must work fast. He slid off Strongheart, with the hair rope and his bow in his hands.

How he wished for arrows with sharp points like the men
hunters and warriors used, instead of the blunt tips which
the young boys of the tribe were given, that were suitable
only for killing small animals.

"Hukahey! Hukahey!" Has-ka yelled the warning cry of
the Sioux when they charged the enemy.

The grizzly dropped to the ground and looked curiously
at this new object which was making such a racket. In
desperation Has-ka quickly fitted one of his blunt-pointed
arrows to his bow, aimed for the bear's eye, drew and let
the arrow fly. There was a terrible roar of rage and pain
from the grizzly as she sat up on her haunches and put her
paws to her nose.

Then Has-ka let out what was certainly a man-sized war
whoop. He had missed the eye, but that blunt arrow had
hit the bear on her tender snout. Quick to take advantage
of this new turn of events, Has-ka folded his rope into a
clout and yelling like a pack of fiends he lunged at the bear,
ready to pound her nose to a pulp. A fierce exultation — a
great rush of power swept through him. He felt strong
enough to battle any grizzly, but at the first blow of the rope
the bear unexpectedly turned to escape from this strange,
noisy, pain-dealing assailant and lumbered into the thicket
roaring as she went. Her two cubs scrambled after her.

Has-ka ran to where his horse, foam-flecked, stood trembling, his headstall caught on a limb. Loosening him, Has-ka
leaped on his back, guided him under the tree and pulled
Little Hawk from his perch.

"We will look for the pony herd tomorrow." Has-ka was still breathing hard and his heart beat against his ribs like a tom-tom. "We must get away from here."

"Let us wait," Little Hawk quavered, "until the grizzly has time to get far away."

"She will not bother us now," Has-ka said. "Not until her bruised nose is healed. She thought we were after her cubs. No wonder she got angry." He knew they would be wise to get far away from this dangerous territory. The strange sense of strength and power was ebbing now and he had no desire to linger in this vicinity.

"You struck the grizzly on the nose!" said Little Hawk in an awe-struck tone as they were riding toward camp. "Our people count coup on a grizzly as they would on an enemy of another tribe."

Has-ka was silent, but the sparkle in his eyes told of his pride. Getting close enough to a living enemy to strike him was considered a braver deed than killing him. Getting close enough to a bear to count coup with a blunt arrow or a rope was something few warriors would care to try. His feat had been a lucky accident; nevertheless, he had done it! Actually doing a thing like this was far better — far more satisfying than dreaming of performing brave deeds.

Yes, what Little Hawk said was true. Their people counted coup on grizzly bear as they would on a human enemy, for the grizzly was the most ferocious of all wild animals. If he had slain the bear, they would let him wear a necklace made of its claws and everyone would look up to him. Only two men in his tribe owned such necklaces.

Perhaps now his father would make him a real coup stick. Maybe he would even paint a picture of him making this coup upon their tepee. Has-ka's mind was filled with big dreams as he rode into camp, dreams which this time were founded on reality.

Little Hawk raced quickly to tell the story to his father, as Has-ka had hoped he would do but had been too proud to suggest. And sure enough, the holy man went among the tepees, as was the Sioux custom, after a memorable deed of a son, shouting, "This day my brave boy, Has-ka, counted coup on the grizzly bear. In honor of his deed I give away my best horse."

That night the old men called Has-ka to the circle around the campfire and asked him to tell of his coup. He stood with the firelight flickering on his acorn-colored skin. "I, Has-ka," he said quietly, "hit the grizzly on the nose with my blunt arrow. Old bear put her hands in front of her face and cried like a papoose. Then I rushed at her with my hair rope and beat her on the nose until she ran away into the woods."

It was just as he had dreamed it so many times. And now it was actually happening. He was standing by the campfire telling of his brave coup, while the other boys sat on the outer edge of the circle staring at him enviously.

"I was there," Little Hawk piped up from the shadows. "I saw what my brother tells about. I saw it."

"Has-ka is brave!" "Has-ka is a credit to his tribe." "Has-ka will be a brave warrior." Murmurs of praise went around the circle and the boy felt lightheaded with happiness, but he modestly acted as if his deed were an everyday happening. Yet when he went to his sleeping robes, that night, never had his dreams of glory been so lofty.

INDIAN
BOY
GROWING
UP

3

HAS-KA ROSE EARLY the next morning. He would go for the pony herd alone, for it was good for an Indian boy to be by himself at times. Twisting his fingers in Strongheart's black mane, he leapt to the horse's back. Today he would offer up a prayer to the Great Spirit in thanks for the new strength and power which had entered his body and soul. Always he had felt himself different from others of his tribe — not only because of his fairer skin and lighter wavy hair — but he was also different in ways he could not describe. No more would this feeling be a disturbing one, for since he had been called by his elders to stand on his feet beside the campfire to tell of his coup on the grizzly bear, this set-apart feeling had taken on new meaning. It was as if Destiny had spoken, telling him that someday he would be great. Perhaps some day the entire Lakota nation would praise him.

"To-kee, Has-ka!" a voice jarred him from his pleasant dream. He glanced down into the handsome, mocking features of No Water who had come from his tepee and was on his way to the stream just as Has-ka was ready to ride forth.

"A fine tale you told last night," he jibed. "Why did you not tell of how you fought the battle of the wasps and ran screaming to the river?"

Has-ka's fine world vanished. His sense of importance flattened like a smashed puffball, yet he managed to stare down at his tormentor with such coolness and contempt that No Water dropped his eyes. Then when Has-ka saw he had outstared him, he pounded his heels against Strongheart's ribs and they galloped off to bring the pony herd back to the village. The cool breeze was welcome against his cheeks still hot from No Water's taunting words, which had jerked back the memory he pushed into the depths of his mind.

"I'll show him!" Has-ka muttered. "Someday the whole Sioux nation will look up to me and call me their leader. I shall be a famous warrior. Braver than the bravest Sioux alive. Braver even than Red Cloud, the warrior they praise so often around the campfire!"

He tensed his muscles with the strength of his resolution. Great as his victory over the bear had been, he knew it would take more than that to make his comrades forget the disgrace of the wasp fight. But he would do it! He would gain their respect and be looked up to as one they would choose as the leader of their games. From there he would go on to greater and greater things.

Has-ka found the pony herd, but he did not stop to commune with *Wakan Tanka,* the Great Spirit. His heart still carried the shame of the battle with the wasps which

No Water's taunts had revived. First he must take the sweat bath and purify himself by fasting before he would be fit to give thanks to the Great Spirit.

Whooping and swinging his arms, he rounded up the ponies and drove them back to the village pole corral. Strongheart worked as if he enjoyed galloping after the strays, wheeling quickly, darting this way and that, while his rider's knees hugged his sides.

Has-ka hobbled his pony outside the village to graze and was walking toward his tepee when he came face to face with High Backbone, the warrior called Hump — Has-ka's hero. The man had a quiver of arrows over his shoulder and was carrying his hunting bow and a buffalo-hair bridle. Evidently he was going on a lone hunt.

Hump stopped and said, "Last night it was good to hear you tell of your coup on the grizzly." He continued without waiting for Has-ka to reply, "Last night I wished you were my son." Then he strode on.

The boy could not have found words had his friend waited. Hump, his hero, had wished that he, Has-ka, were his son! How many times he had hoped the Hump would adopt him and teach him the ways of a warrior. His real son and namesake was one of Has-ka's best friends.

His own father, the holy man, was well thought of and counseled those who asked for advice, but he was not a warrior and had no wish that either of his sons should be warriors. Has-ka, however, had made up his own mind about his future; now he was determined to win recognition as a brave.

His ambition made him restless and the summer days drifted by too slowly for an impatient boy. Village life was quiet. The women tanned skins from the last hunt. The men made arrows, lounged against their backboards, or simply basked in the sun and talked. There were no battles with enemy tribes or even pony stealing expeditions against the Crows. The valley drowsed beneath the blazing sun and still skies. But life was never really dull for an Indian boy. Each day there was a hunt of some sort. Each day had its own kind of excitement.

Secretly Has-ka was making himself some sharp-tipped arrows. He might have slain the grizzly bear had he been properly armed. He had made up his mind then to be prepared for any dangerous adventure, but he did not want anyone to know that he was making himself a warrior's weapons for fear he would be laughed at for his high aspirations.

Evenings around the tepee fire his father or his grandfather told of some past deed of the Sioux. Then Has-ka was called upon to repeat the story of the evening before. In this way he learned the history of his family and his tribe.

It made him proud to hear the tales of the greatness of his people. He learned that the Lakota Sioux of which his own Oglala tribe was a part, were the greatest of all the Indian nations — the bravest in war; the wisest in peace; the strongest in mind and body.

The Oglalas moved about with the changing seasons. Sometimes they hunted buffaloes on the wide Laramie Plains. Sometimes they moved to the Big Horn Mountains for deer and elk, for the fun of stealing horses from the Crows — or for the glory of counting coup upon this long-time enemy tribe.

Each season had its experiences which developed in the young Indian boy the qualities important to a warrior. Often there were times when Has-ka became impatient with the slowness of his own development. His body was grow-

ing taller and his muscles stronger but still he was not as
stalwart as he wished to be. He was still slim and smaller
than most boys his age. The resolution to become a hero
which had followed the shameful conduct during the battle
with the wasps had never wavered. In fact, it grew stronger
with each passing season — yet sometimes months went by
with no progress toward his goal. True, he was seldom
taunted now about the wasp episode. No Water seemed to
be the only one who remembered it and who deliberately
tried to keep the memory alive among the Oglala boys.

Gradually it dawned upon Has-ka that No Water was
envious of him — regarded him as a rival in certain abilities
and the realization filled Has-ka's heart with satisfaction,
for the older boy was outstanding in the tribe.

There was still only one skill in which Has-ka was the
champion — that of horsemanship. The ability to ride well
was an all-important one to the Plains Indian, and it was
one which Sioux boys practiced industriously, both for the
fun of it, and as something that would later make them
better warriors.

Everyone in the village came out to watch when the
Oglala boys put on a riding contest. Each boy galloped by
the line of spectators, displaying every feat of horsemanship at his command. The main object was to make themselves "invisible" to the "enemy," (the spectators) by
riding low on the side of the horse. Has-ka was able to do
this with only a heel showing over Strongheart's neck.

"Has-ka is invisible." "Has-ka is the best rider," the
watchers cried.

The pride he always felt when praised for his horsemanship was very agreeable and he often deliberately attracted
attention by running beside the galloping Strongheart
through the center of the village, then leaping to his back

by grasping mane or tail. None of the other boys could
perform such a feat.

Has-ka was also a swift runner. Nearly every day there
was a foot race among the camp boys. Sometimes Has-ka
won and sometimes No Water did, but always the rivalry
between the two boys was keen and none too friendly, and
every time Has-ka won, No Water opened up the old sore
spot. The younger boy longed for something to happen that
would put his rival in a similar unfavorable position, but
nothing did.

No Water was a better swimmer, a better wrestler, he
could shoot his bow much farther — and most painful of
all to Has-ka's pride, he was often chosen for leader in mock
battles and contests. Often in moments of discouragement
it seemed to him that he was no nearer his goal of becoming
great among the Sioux than he was when his resolution was
made.

Things came so easily to No Water — almost without
effort it seemed. Why should his own path be so difficult?
Yet he had several steadfast friends who chose his comrade-
ship rather than that of the more spectacular No Water. It
was consoling to think of them. He Dog, also a quiet,
serious boy, was the one most similar to himself in actions
and interests. When they were together there were long
silences, but Has-ka found greater satisfaction in his companionship than that of any other boy.

Young Hump was a restless, active boy, always in search
of adventure and one whose voice was loud in calling attention to Has-ka's accomplishments.

Lone Bear often tagged along with them, making them
laugh because of his clumsiness. Yet they were sometimes
impatient with him, too, because he could not be quick
and quiet in his movements, but had a habit of stumbling

over his feet, as the *heyoka* (clown) did on purpose, or of getting tangled in the rope when he tried to catch his horse.

Two other boys who were usually together often joined Has-ka's group. Touch-the-Clouds was thin and so tall that he towered over his companions; Little Big Man was shorter than anyone his age, but his sturdiness and strength made up for his lack of height.

Has-ka knew that this handful of boys liked and respected him. It was a start toward leadership and gave him a measure of confidence — but he still had that set-apart, alone feeling.

Often he wondered about his hero, High Backbone, his friend's father, the warrior called Hump. He remembered how Hump had said once that he might adopt him as his son to teach him the secrets of warfare. But nothing more had happened. Often Has-ka was aware of Hump's eyes following him, as though studying him — trying to read what was in his mind. Had the warrior forgotten his half-promise, Has-ka wondered — or was he disappointed because he had not made faster progress?

Early one morning, the village was bustling with the exciting news of a great herd of buffalo which a scout had seen some miles to the south. The ponies were hurriedly driven into the corral near the village. As all the hunters rode bareback it was but a short time until a hunting party galloped toward the buffalo. The men were armed with bows and arrows or lances. Three of them had the white man's thunder sticks. Eager to be in on the buffalo hunt, his first, Has-ka, on Strongheart, raced after the band. He carried his own ash bow, his new, sharp-tipped arrows and a bone skinning knife. The party left the village with Hump at its head, because among all the Sioux, he was the greatest hunter.

They rode until the sun was past the middle. Then Has-ka saw Hump raise his hand and by spreading his arms and bringing them forward, indicate the party was to form a line and ride up abreast of him. Has-ka had not yet seen the buffalo but he knew the advanced rider had and he guided his pony to get into position.

No sooner had the line formed than Hump started the chase, sending his men to "make the surround" of the herd. At first the buffalo seemed unaware of the hunters but when they got the man-scent, a few started milling and running. It was but a very short time until the whole herd broke into motion like prairie grass struck by a sudden gust of wind.

A shrill "Hi-yi-yi!" ripped from Has-ka's throat. Every nerve was tense with excitement. Strongheart got the spirit of the run and scarcely seemed to touch the ground, so fast did he go as the boy kneed him close to the plunging herd. A wave of heat from the sweating bodies struck him. He could smell the strong animal odor and feel the brush of coarse hair against his bare leg. The dust blinded and suffocated him. Clods thrown by pounding hoofs hit his face and it was not until he had ridden past a large portion of the stampeding herd that he remembered he was there not only to chase buffalo but to kill them.

Leaning low along Strongheart's neck, Has-ka peered through the cloud of dust trying to spot a fat young animal. He saw one just beyond a big shaggy bull. Quickly he fitted an arrow to his bow and pulled with all his strength, aiming behind the animal's shoulder. The arrow found its mark but the animal kept on running as if it had not been hit. Quickly again he fitted arrow to bow, determined that this time his shot would be true — the shaggy beast would not ignore it.

Intent on getting into position to shoot again, Has-ka

did not notice that Strongheart had worked his way inside the herd and that he and his horse were hemmed in by stampeding buffalo. But he realized this quickly enough when plunging animals crowded his legs so close to Strongheart's sides that Has-ka thought they would surely be crushed. But no matter what happened, he must stick to his horse's back. The stories he had heard of hunters' being trampled beneath thundering hoofs flashed through his mind.

On, on they pounded. If only Strongheart would keep his footing! If he should step in a prairie dog hole and hurtle Has-ka over his head. . . . The boy shuddered. There was only one hope. He pulled with all his might on Strongheart's mane — the signal for him to slow down, but this was impossible to do with buffalo crowding them from the rear. At last, however, the herd began to thin as the great beasts thundered past. Now, finally only a few stragglers plunged by them and Has-ka could breathe again.

When fear eased slowly from his brain, disappointment took its place. Disappointment that he had not made a kill. Then through the dust he spied a lumbering beast, evidently wounded and unable to keep up with the herd. Kneeing Strongheart closer, he saw that it was the animal he had shot. It was his own arrow protruding from behind its shoulder. Again he quickly fitted arrow to bow and fired, again his arrow found its mark but did not bring the animal down. Enraged, it turned with a bellow, head down, snorting, and charged head on to gore Strongheart.

Pounding the stallion's neck to get him to wheel out of the path of the pain-crazed beast, Has-ka felt the sharp horn tear across his leg. Again the buffalo lunged. Strongheart was hard put to turn sharply enough to avoid those cruel horns. He was winded.

A cry rose to Has-ka's lips. This time the buffalo was going to gore Strongheart. It was the end! Then suddenly the shaggy beast's legs buckled under it. Its snout plowed into the ground. It rose shakily again, shook its head, made a few steps forward, then with a giant sigh it sank slowly to rise no more.

What had happened?

A figure rode out of the cloud of dust, left by the thundering herd. It was Hump, the hunter, on his white horse.

Has-ka stared down in bewilderment at the fallen buffalo. The point of an arrow protruded, close to the spot where his own had gone in. Then slowly it dawned upon him. So that was what had happened! Hump with his longer bow and greater strength had shot the buffalo from the opposite side and his arrow had gone clear through the great body.

The boy grinned his thanks to his friend. Words did not come easily to his lips, and in this case they were not necessary.

The warrior, however, was stern. "Only a foolish one would ride among buffalo," he scolded. "Being foolish is not being brave. You must have a stronger bow. Hump himself will make it for you. And Hump will teach you the ways of the Sioux warrior and hunter. Your heart is strong, but your sense is weak."

Has-ka's joy and gratitude shone from his eyes. Hump was really making him his son! One dream had come true. Now he would also make his dream of becoming a great hunter and warrior come true. With Hump to show him the way, he could not fail.

Has-ka slid from the winded Strongheart and limped to the buffalo. Hump examined Has-ka's leg where the buffalo's horn had torn across it. It was not a serious wound, although it would be painful for a few days.

Hump showed Has-ka how to butcher the great animal, slitting the skin down the belly and the insides of the legs. Bracing his feet against the carcass, he started at the chest and pulled the skin off like a glove. Next, with Hump's white man's knife and Has-ka's stone one they cut the meat with the grain of the big muscles so that the women could slice it into thin strips for drying. Has-ka helped with this work to the utmost of his strength.

When the butchering was done, Hump spread the hide, hair down, on Strongheart's back, then they lifted the meat onto it, pulling the edges of the hide together to cover the meat. The horse was almost hidden and Has-ka must limp back to camp.

While they waited for Strongheart to take a brief breathing spell, Has-ka and Hump carefully turned the skull of the buffalo so that it would face the rising sun.

"This service we do for Pte, our uncle, the buffalo," Hump said solemnly. "The services he does for us are many as the leaves of the aspen. Without him we would die."

Has-ka was well-satisfied with himself as he led Strongheart toward the camp. How pleased his mother would be with all of this meat and this fine large hide to tan for clothing, for weapons, and ornaments. Tonight again the men would talk about him at the campfire meeting, for he was the youngest one who had gone on the hunt.

THE
EARNED
NAME

■■■■■■■ 4

As THE HUNTERS rode into the Oglala village, laughing and jabbering, the Indian women came out to meet them and ran beside their horses. Has-ka's sister, Laughing One, and his stepmother, Gathers-Her-Berries, ran beside his horse chattering like magpies over his kill.

Reaching camp the women seized the meat and threw the hunks onto beds of leaves while they deftly sliced it into strips which they threw over pole racks to dry, out of reach of the dogs.

That night the campfires sputtered and blazed as the buffalo fat dripped onto them. The air was savory with fine smells of roasting hump and ribs. The Oglalas ate until they were stuffed. Never had food tasted so good to Has-ka. The fact that he had helped in providing meat for the camp made him feel pleasantly important and he was still elated over the fact that Hump had singled him out.

He purposely walked through the camp to see if he would be noticed. He was. Men pointed to him and said, "There goes Has-ka. His arrow brought down a buffalo. He was the youngest one on the hunt."

It was very agreeable to be pointed out and noticed this way. He almost forgot that Hump had to come to his rescue just in time.

When the Oglalas had eaten so much that they could not cram down another mouthful, they danced to the throbbing drums until the food was jounced down enough so that they could eat some more. Has-ka ate and danced with them. He was aware of No Water's glowering, envious glances upon him but this only increased his feeling of triumph. The older boy had gone along on the hunt, but only as one of the boys who led a pack horse on which to bring back the meat. He had had no part in the kill and no one after the hunt had pointed him out as he walked through the village.

Has-ka gorged himself and danced until he grew so sleepy that he crawled off to his sleeping robes. However, he was up at dawn the next morning, eager for more excitement.

Mock buffalo hunts were always a favorite pastime of Sioux youngsters. After one of the real hunts there were often buffalo calves left behind on the plains, which had been unable to keep up with the herd after it had been stampeded. It was the delight of the boys to chase these calves, shooting at them with the blunt arrows they used in their games.

Has-ka, filled with elation over his first buffalo hunt, joined in the noisy horseback chase of one of these young calves. Strongheart was the first to catch up with it. With a yell of triumph the boy shouted, "I, Has-ka the buffalo hunter, will ride this calf!"

Leaning over, he grabbed a handful of the woolly hair of the hump and threw himself onto the calf's back. More frightened than ever by this new terror, the young buffalo increased his speed so that the Indian boys' ponies could scarcely keep up. But what they lacked in speed, they made up for in yelling as they gave chase.

The calf suddenly stopped running and tried by bucking to rid itself of the strange and frightening thing clinging to its back. Has-ka found this change of pace not at all to his liking. His head was rammed down between his shoulders. With each jump that jounced him first to one side, then to the other, he thought he could not stick on, but he righted himself and managed. His companions were not going to be given a chance to laugh at him. He must not lose the importance he had gained. Most of all he dreaded giving No Water another opportunity to ridicule him. Once he was tipped clear over to the side of the calf. It was only the realization of how his comrades would whoop with glee if he were thrown that gave him the determination to right himself and hang grimly on.

Gradually the bucking eased off, then ceased, when the calf became tired.

"I, Has-ka, did ride the buffalo calf," he cried, raising his hand in triumph.

"Has-ka did ride the buffalo calf," his companions chanted.

"I, Has-ka, will ride the buffalo calf into the village," he shouted.

"*Hoka hey! Hoka hey!*" his friends cried, crowding their ponies close to the buffalo calf and driving it toward the Oglala camp. The riderless Strongheart trotted at the rear of the yelling horde.

Drawn by the shouts of the boys the people came from

their tepees to see the procession led by young Has-ka riding the buffalo calf.

"Has-ka did ride the buffalo calf!" his friends shouted.

The warrior Hump stood in front of his lodge laughing at the sight. "The buffalo calf seems too tame a mount for you, my friend," he said.

"He was wild enough out there on the hills," young Hump said. "You should have seen Has-ka ride. I thought the calf's bucking would snap his head off as we snap off the head of a grouse."

"It was easy," Has-ka said modestly. A new hope, however, was born within him that his people would now give him a man-like earned name such as Rides the Buffalo Calf instead of the one he so detested.

But the next day he was still called Has-ka.

The incident, though, did reawaken Hump's interest in him and the warrior made him his adopted son, according to the Sioux custom, and taught him the lore of his people, the best way to make weapons and the secrets of warfare, finding in the eager boy an apt pupil.

His own son, young Hump, was restless and had not Has-ka's ambition to become a leader and his father often lost patience with him. The warrior and his pupil, however, were so often together that their tribesmen spoke of them as the "grizzly and his cub."

Was ever another boy so fortunate, Has-ka wondered, as to have so fine a teacher? In every way he strove to make himself like his hero. Yet he never found courage to speak to Hump of his high ambitions for fear of being laughed at. The man, however, at times possessed an uncanny ability to sense what was in the boy's mind.

One day they were returning from a hunt, jogging along in silence. Has-ka had been completely lost in his thoughts,

imagining himself leading a band of Oglala warriors against the Crow tribe.

Suddenly Hump said, "To be a leader of your people you must listen often and in silence to the Great Holy Mystery. The day is not too far away when you will go alone to the hills for the Vision Quest."

Has-ka looked startled. He was surprised that Hump knew what was in his mind, and it pleased him that his teacher considered him worthy of the test which would prove whether or not the *Wakan Tanka* would guide him to leadership.

"You think — I may someday be a leader?" Has-ka's tone was hopeful.

Hump gave him a long, strange look, and for a moment did not speak. Finally he said, "The desire for prominence among our people is always in your heart. Why?"

Has-ka met his friend's glance with a questioning look.

"Why?" Hump asked again. "Why is the wish for greatness always with you?"

"Because — " Haska floundered for words. "It is a good thing to be great. To be pointed out. To be a leader — "

It was not easy to put into words the reasons for his deepest desire. A shadow of disappointment crossed the warrior's face and Has-ka saw that he was not pleased.

"Your reasons are selfish ones," Hump's tone was harsh. "Leadership is a gift from the *Wakan Tanka*. To be used for the good of the people — not because one would be pointed out."

Has-ka felt humbled. "How does one know if he is singled out for leadership — to serve his people?" he persisted.

"At the time of the Vision Quest," Hump repeated. "It is time you were thinking about getting ready."

As the preliminary step of training for the sterner ordeal ahead, Hump one day ordered him to do without food for an entire day. The warrior blackened Has-ka's face with charred wood as the sign that he was fasting. His comrades pranced about him, tantalizing him by holding juicy chunks of savory buffalo meat close to his mouth, or by offering him *wasna*, dried ground buffalo meat mixed with ground-up plums — a favorite food of the Indians.

He wore a solemn expression on his blackened face as he went about the camp. The holy, set-apart feeling he had today was very pleasant — not like the old set-apart feeling he used to have because of his light complexion and his lack of sureness in himself. In those days the feeling had been so painful and unbearable sometimes that he had wanted to crawl off like a wounded animal.

He kept to himself the entire day, not being in a mood

to join the other boys in their rough fun. He wandered along Lodge Pole Creek, then lay on the warm grass with his hands under his head, staring at the lazy clouds floating above him until he drifted off into deep sleep. In his dreams he saw himself single-handed driving off the pony herds of the enemy — slaying enemy chiefs — saving his hero, Hump, from the scalping knife. He saw himself being called upon to stand up beside the campfire to tell of his remarkable coups. Saw his record being painted upon a white buffalo robe. Saw the feathered crown of a chieftain being placed upon his head.

When he awoke he struggled to recapture those pleasant dreams, but now he was wide awake. He got to his feet and strolled along the stream, then wandered to the top of a hill. By now the sun was dipping beyond the western horizon in a blaze of brilliant colors. Lightheaded from hunger, Has-ka stretched his hands toward the sinking sun. "A vision, *Wakan Tanka,*" he murmured. "Grant me a vision of greatness. Show me the path I must take."

In his dizzy, elated state he fully expected the golden clouds to part, revealing the *Wakan Tanka.* — Or the Holy Mystery would send one of His animal spirits with a message telling Has-ka that he was truly destined for greatness and that he would be powerful among the Sioux. All of the men who were leaders among Has-ka's people had received such visions or messages at some time or other — usually following a fast.

He stood until his outstretched arms ached — and his soul ached, too, with the waiting. But no vision — no message came. The sun sank. A veil of darkness fell over the world, and Has-ka's spirits sank with the sun. Perhaps he was not destined for greatness after all! His arms fell to his sides and he walked slowly back to the village.

Two sleeps following Has-ka's fast, No Water raced through the village shouting, "*Che-hoo-hoo! Che-hoo-hoo!* All who are brave and strong, line up for *che-hoo-hoo*."

This was a wrestling game in which the Sioux boys chose sides, each boy picking his own opponent. When a wrestler's shoulders were forced to the ground, he was "dead."

Young Hump was one of the leaders; No Water, as usual, was the other. Hump chose Has-ka to be on his side. Has-ka looked over the "enemy" line to pick out someone about his own size and weight to challenge.

He was startled when he heard No Water shout his own name.

"I, No Water," the enemy leader yelled, "do challenge the One Who Cries When the Wasps Sting Him."

The older boy could not have chosen a surer way of arousing Has-ka to anger than with this almost-forgotten taunt. Sudden fury boiled through his veins, yet he was no fool. No Water was larger and heavier — had every chance of winning. But, of course, he had to accept the challenge or be disgraced in the eyes of his comrades.

Soon enemy was upon enemy and the ground was covered with writhing, struggling pairs. Has-ka braced himself as No Water seized him. He fought with every ounce of strength that was in him and when his breath rasped in his throat and he was so exhausted that every muscle felt limp, he gritted his teeth and kept on struggling and straining until unknown reserves of strength came to his help. But grit and determination were not sufficient against superior strength and weight.

At last when many shoulders were pinned to the ground, the victors pretended to take the scalps of those whom they had defeated. It was not until most of the pairs had ended their struggles that No Water managed to throw Has-ka and leap upon him to pin his shoulders to the ground. According to the rules of the game that was supposed to be the end of it, except for the pretended scalping, but No Water knelt on Has-ka's shoulders while his thumbs pressed the beaten boy's windpipe.

Has-ka's breath came out with a gurgling groan — almost a cry. His good friend, He Dog, pulled No Water off.

The *che-hoo-hoo* winners danced the victory dance about the defeated enemy who hunched sullenly in the center of the ring. No Water pointed triumphantly to Has-ka and shouted, "*Hopo!* I, No Water, did beat my enemy He-Who-Cries-When-the-Wasps-Sting. And I did make him cry out again. Has-ka has not the brave heart! Has-ka is a girl!"

The beaten boy's spirits sank to his moccasins. He had thought he was making headway in gaining the respect of his comrades. Now, even though he had done his best, he had disgraced himself again. He had given his rival another chance to gloat over him. Why did the older boy hate him so? Why did he always try to belittle him before his companions?

Disgraced and unhappy Has-ka shunned his comrades until an exciting event made him forget his personal troubles.

An unknown disease had swept through the pony herd the previous winter and there was talk of the need of new horses. Has-ka listened eagerly. He hoped that a pony-stealing expedition was afoot.

The easiest method of acquiring new horses and the one the Sioux liked best because of the excitement it afforded, was to creep at night into some camp of their enemy, the Crows, and drive their tamed horses away. But now the Crows were far beyond the Big Horns, so the Oglalas must round up wild horses to replenish their herds. This method was harder work, for the horses so caught must be broken and the Sioux would be denied the sly pleasure of besting the enemy Crows.

An excited longing swept through Has-ka as he listened to the plans for the wild horse hunt. He made up his mind to go along.

Nearly all of the men, and some of the boys who were old enough, joined the wild horse hunt. Scouts rode out ahead toward the sand hills to see if they could locate a herd of wild horses and after riding for nearly half a sun they gave the blanket signal from a hilltop that they had discovered a herd in the valley below. The Indians scattered, circling the valley, but staying out of sight of the horses. Has-ka was riding Strongheart. He quivered with excitement as his group waited beneath the brow of the hill for the signal to advance.

When the surround was complete, several of the hunters on the south side rode over the hill yelling. The wild horses stampeded in the opposite direction, where Has-ka and his companions were waiting. Some of the hunters strung out across their path. The horses galloped in another direction only to have more hunters block their way. Finding every direction of escape closed to them, the frightened, bewildered animals started circling. When they were milling in a compact bunch, the hunters closed in on them and started thrusting their long sticks with hair rope loops over the heads of the horses they wanted to capture.

Has-ka caught sight of a pony the color of a red autumn leaf. It carried its small, well-shaped head high, nostrils distended. Its eyes were wide open but there was more a look of fight in them than of fear. The instant he saw the red stallion, Has-ka knew that it was a spirited and intelligent animal and he wanted it with all of his heart. So also

did Lone Bear and he thrust out his loop trying to get it over the animal's head, but missed. Has-ka thrust out his loop, but he missed, too, for even though the red horse was frightened he was wise and wary.

Finally Lone Bear gave up with a grunt of disgust and concentrated his efforts on a less crafty animal, but no other would satisfy Has-ka. Already some of his comrades were riding toward home trailing their mustangs, which they called crazy horses, tied to the tails of their tame ponies.

At last his loop settled over the neck of the red horse and with a yell of triumph he jerked on the willow pole, drawing the loop tight. The animal reared and snorted, but could not rid itself of the thing around its neck that was fast choking its breath from it.

Has-ka edged Strongheart close to the wild pony and then he did a daring thing. He threw himself onto the red pony's back, with nothing in the world with which to control it but the hair loop around its neck.

With a shrill whinny of rebellion the red horse broke loose from the herd, galloped into the open, bucking, rearing, turning, twisting, omitting none of the tricks a wild horse knows in an effort to dislodge its rider. He sunfished and galloped, but Has-ka clung to his mane, tightening the noose around its neck when necessary, but giving the magnificent animal its head as much as possible. A wild sense of elation swept through the boy. He yelled and his heels pounded the sides of the wild horse. He would ride this horse and finally conquer him.

The hunters stopped trying to capture mustangs to watch the performance that went on all over the hillside between Has-ka and the wild horse, until it was flecked with foam and finally stood with drooping head and heaving sides, too spent to struggle longer. It recognized a master.

Has-ka was spent, too, yet a thrill of triumph swept through him. He had conquered this splendid beast. Loosening his noose he reached forward and grasping an ear he turned the pony's head, his heels pounding its sides. Slowly the red pony obeyed his master's will and stumbled in the direction Has-ka wanted him to go.

When Has-ka, astride the horse he had conquered, rode up to his companions, they shouted, "He has ridden a crazy horse! *Tashunka-Witko!* Crazy Horse! Crazy Horse! His name shall be *Tashunka-Witko!* Crazy Horse!"

The boy's heart beat faster. At last he had an earned name — and a splendid one. The name of his father, but one which he himself had earned. To the Indians the name meant an untamed, splendid horse of great spirit and courage. He could not have earned a finer name, even if he had chosen it.

Crazy Horse made his rope into a halter and tied the horse to Strongheart's tail. Neither animal liked being tied to the other, but Strongheart was trained to obey and the wild horse was tired, so they got along well enough.

When the horse hunters reached their village, the first thing they did was to rope and throw the mustangs they had captured. The right fore foot was tied to the left hind foot and the horse allowed to struggle to his feet. Now the ponies could not kick and the process of taming them started at once.

Every day Crazy Horse went to the corral and roped this new horse he named Warrior. He stroked him and talked to him, breaking and training him as he had Strongheart, until finally the spirited pony yielded to the stronger will. Crazy Horse grinned with pleasure, for there were not two finer ponies in the Oglala camp than Strongheart and Warrior — and well he knew there wasn't a better horseman.

Never was there a day when the boys of Crazy Horse's band were not practicing riding in some form or other. There were races in the early evening, but Crazy Horse's favorite sport and the one he always wanted was the riding contest in which the boys chose sides. When Crazy Horse would gallop his stallion at its utmost speed, past his admiring companions, making it zigzag in its course, with just the tip of his heel showing over its neck, they would cry, "*Tashunka-Witko* — Crazy Horse rides without being seen!" "Crazy Horse was invisible to the enemy!" "Crazy Horse is the finest rider in the Oglala camp!"

■■■■■■■■■■■

BLOOD
ON
THE
PLAINS
■■■■■■■■ 5

IT WAS THE MONTH when the Plums Turn Ripe. Haze lay over the plains and Laramie Peak loomed like a serene blue sentinel, while Shell River gleamed in the sun. The Oglala village dozed in the heat, with the sides of the tepees rolled up to catch any vagrant breeze. Eagle-wing fans moved slowly in old men's hands. Most of the women and girls were off in the hills picking the choke cherries which loaded the bushes to the ground with the purplish, shining fruit.

Young Crazy Horse sat cross-legged before Hump's lodge, making a strong bow from a piece of ash under the supervision of his teacher. He Dog, Touch-the-Clouds, and Lone Bear sauntered by and asked the boy to go to swim in the river, but he shook his head. When the bow was finished and the string had been tightened to give it the right curve, Hump tested it with one of his own arrows, giving a grunt of satisfaction indicating that it had sufficient spring and force.

"Try it," he said, handing the bow to Crazy Horse along with an arrow.

The boy quickly raised the bow and let the arrow fly. It landed on a straight line with the one which Hump had shot, but not so far.

Crazy Horse's eye shone. "*Was-te!* Good!" he said. "No other boy in the Oglala camp has such a fine bow."

Hump rose and stepped into the tepee, coming out in a moment with a fine quiver made of otter skin. "This I have made for you myself, my son, and I give it to you as a present from your teacher."

Crazy Horse thrust his arrows into the quiver and stretched the string of his bow.

"Now," he said after a moment of silence, "I am ready to be a warrior."

He raised his eyes until they were on a level with Hump's breast, where the slanting scars of the Sun Dance stood out. He wondered if someday he would be able to endure without flinching or fainting the tortures of the Sun Dance.

"*Are* you ready?" Hump asked quietly. "It takes more than a strong bow and a quiver full of arrows to make a warrior."

Crazy Horse lifted his eyes still farther, to meet Hump's own. "I have much to learn," he said humbly.

"*Hau*," Hump agreed, "but you have a fine spirit. Practice hard. You will learn."

The sun was dipping low. It was the time of day for eating meat. Hump turned without further speech and went into his lodge. Crazy Horse walked swiftly toward his own tepee. The sky singers rose toward the heavens, dripping song as they went and his spirits soared with them.

Hump had said that he, Crazy Horse, would learn. He had the spirit of a fine warrior. *Hoye!* Hump's words gave him such a sense of power that he longed for opportunities to prove himself.

Life was good in the Shell River camp. From the high bluffs Crazy Horse could watch antelope run across the plains, looking like shadows of clouds. There were prairie chickens, curlew, deer and antelope upon which he could practice marksmanship with his new bow, and which helped the family stew pot.

But now the Oglalas were breaking camp — moving down from the hills to the white man's place called Fort Laramie. Messengers from the fort had asked all of the Sioux to come to a great council. There was something about a paper to sign concerning the white man's crossing the land of the Sioux, and a promise of many presents from the Great White Father in Washington.

Crazy Horse heard much talk around the campfires about this paper. Many of the Oglalas had been to Fort Laramie which had been built by the white fur traders who lived like the Indian, spoke with the straight tongue, and who married Indian women. Now, however, the soldiers had taken over the fort and had sent the traders to Jim Bordeaux's stone house down the river. It was the soldiers who had sent the Sioux the invitation to the big council on the Platte.

Crazy Horse had never seen the fort and he was eager for the trek. "It is on the land the Great Spirit gave to us from which we drove the Cheyennes and Pawnees," said Hump. "It is like an island of white men in an ocean of Lakotas."

Chief Brave Bear gave the word to move and early in the morning the women took down the tepees and rolled them into packs to be put upon travois, with the tepee poles tied across them. Other travois were piled with household goods. Before the sun was halfway to the middle, the village was on the move.

Brave Bear, Bull Tail, Man-Afraid-of-His-Horses and Hump rode out in front. Behind them came the subchiefs and counselors, among them the older Crazy Horse. A few of the *akicita*, police, came next, followed by the old men, the women and the children. The warriors with bows, lances and war clubs flanked the column, at the end of which trailed the travois and pony herd.

The women and girls were dressed in their best white deerskin embroidered with colored porcupine quills, their faces painted with vermilion. Dogs yapped and boys, yelling like fiends, raced their horses up and down the column. Crazy Horse showed off his horsemanship, galloping Strongheart, then sliding off over his rump and vaulting to his back again, or riding against the stallion's side with only a heel showing over his neck. When Strongheart tired he put him with the pony herd and climbed on Warrior who was always ready for a race. Although he pretended not to notice, he was well aware of the shy but admiring glances that many of the girls cast in his direction — especially of the one called Her-Black-Robe. She was as slim and straight as an arrow, with hair as shining black as the wing of a crow and her dark eyes were as soft and shy as those of a fawn. For several moons now Crazy Horse had been conscious of her veiled glances.

When the leaders signaled that Fort Laramie was just over the next rise, Crazy Horse galloped ahead to see. Never had he seen such a fine sight as that glistening white adobe fort squatting on the prairie with Laramie Peak standing guard and the Black Hills looming in the distance. Surrounding the fort were thousands of painted tepees and the ponies on the hillsides were as thick as the grasshoppers that made the ground bare.

Now would follow a great time of eating, of dancing, or races and games and tales of brave deeds to be painted on robes by the picture man.

Around the council fires Crazy Horse heard the loud arguments between the men. Arguments concerning the coming of the white men in their wagons across the land of the Sioux. The boy did not pay much attention to the talk, but he gathered that the soldiers at the fort wanted the head men of the Sioux to put their hands to a stick, making black marks on a piece of white paper. By so doing they would promise not to harm the white men who crossed in wagons over the Holy Road joining the lands of the rising and setting sun — the road the whites called the Laramie Trail, but which the Indians called holy because those who traveled it must not be molested. In exchange for this promise, each year in the Moon of Falling Leaves the Great White Father in Washington would send wagon loads of food and gifts to his red children.

Brave Bear, chief of the Oglalas, was an old man and tired of hunting. The soldiers piled his travois with bright blankets, with food, with beads and papers of vermilion for his women. They decked him out in a blue soldier's coat with shiny brass buttons and gave him a soldier's hat. He cut the top out of the hat so that his eagle feathers could poke through and he did not bother to wear the trousers they gave him; his breechclout was enough. His bony legs under the too-big coat looked like those of a heron and made the children snicker at the sight, but he thought he looked very fine and strutted whenever he wore his new outfit.

The soldiers told him that he was a "good" Indian because he was willing to do all that they asked and they gave

him a piece of paper saying that they had made him "Chief of all the Sioux."

Crazy Horse heard his people laugh at this bit of news. He knew that no white man could make an Indian a chief — only his own band had that power. And, of course, only a great council of all of the numerous tribes and bands could make any man chief of all the Lakotas. Only a very great man would merit such an honor, and Brave Bear was not great. Certainly not since he had bowed so easily to the will of the Blue Coats. The young braves held him in contempt, because of his silly strutting around in his blue soldier coat. The old men who were tired of fighting and hunting sided with Brave Bear and said that there was grass and game enough for all. "Let the white men follow their road in peace. Life around Fort Laramie was pleasant and would be easy with the White Father's food and presents coming in each Moon of the Falling Leaves."

Upon hearing such talk, Red Cloud, one of the brave young warriors, rose to his feet beside the campfire.

"Are we to be like women — to sit around the fort of the Blue Coats waiting for presents?" he cried. "Beggars, Loafers-Around-the-Fort? Let us move into the hunting country. Let us drive the stinking whites from the Holy Road. Let us act like Indian braves."

"*Haye! Haye!*" the young men chorused.

Brave Bear, the "Paper Chief," rose to his feet all in a fluster and held out his hands as if to soothe his tribesmen.

"There is land enough for all," he said. "Let us remain friends with the white men."

Red Cloud spat out, "White men speak with crooked tongues. Let the Loafers-Around-the-Fort stay. Those of the brave heart follow me."

Many of the young men rode with him, away toward the mountains to hunt, steal ponies and do the other things that made life worth living.

Crazy Horse sighed as he watched them ride away. He was becoming restless from inaction. Visiting back and forth between camps, games and races were all very well for a time, but an Indian was created for sterner, more exciting things. He did not want the life of his fathers to change. Already some of his people were imitating the ways of the white men — wearing the white men's clothes, eating their food — and when they could get it, even drinking their fire water which made fools of the strongest braves.

It was when such a mood of restlessness was upon him

that he decided to visit the near-by Brulé camp. His father was an Oglala, but his dead mother had been a Brulé, so it would be pleasant he thought, to spend a time with his mother's people.

He braided his hair with strips of otter skin, put on the moccasins his sister had trimmed with gay beads, gifts of the white man, and his fringed breechclout. He usually rode bareback, but for this visit he put a saddle onto Strongheart's back. The saddle was made of a piece of folded moosehide with the hair inside and riding on it was like riding upon a springy pillow. He took his new bow and filled the otter skin with arrows and rode proudly into the Brulé camp.

His mother's relatives gathered around him in noisy welcome and gave him the most comfortable place in the lodge and the first choice of meat in the hide stew pot.

But in spite of the races and games and exchange of news, life after a few sleeps became as dull as it had been at his own camp and he longed for excitement. It came — very suddenly and with much force.

Emigrants of the band the whites called Mormons were straggling over the Holy Road. Crazy Horse and several Brulé boys were having a horse race. They frightened a skinny, footsore cow trailing the Mormon caravan. This cow stampeded straight through the Brulé camp and into the lodge of Chief Mat-to-i-o-way, upsetting the pot of buffalo stew, knocking over the pole bearing the hide on which Mat-to-i-o-way's coups were pictured and even tearing a great gash in one side of the lodge.

It was a comical sight that made Crazy Horse and his companions double up with laughter. The Mormons went on without stopping to offer presents for the damage done to the chief — but no matter. White people were like that.

The Brulés tied the animal to a lodge pole and waited for the white owner to come back and claim it. But the cow was a worn-out creature, stringy, footsore and thin, with all of its ribs showing — not worth coming back after.

When no one claimed it, Straight Foretop, a visiting Miniconjou, butchered the animal and the meat was divided among the lodges to be dropped into the stew pots.

Crazy Horse did not eat any of the meat; as a guest he was entitled to more choice fare. But Mat-to-i-o-way gave him a piece of the hide with which to make a war club.

The next day the fat fur trader, Bordeaux, who was married to a Brulé woman, rode into the village. "The Mormons are making bad talk at the fort," he said, "about you stealing a cow. You must take it to the Mormons or they will make trouble."

"It is too late to give back the cow," Mat-to-i-o-way shrugged. "It is already eaten. And stringy, stinking stuff it was."

He wrinkled up his nose at the memory of the bad-smelling meat, and Crazy Horse in sympathy wrinkled his nose, too, although he hadn't eaten any. But the odor of the white men's cattle was as repugnant to him as it was to all Indians. That was not surprising, however, because the white men themselves had a peculiar and disgusting smell.

"Oh, well!" Bordeaux said. "It isn't a matter of too much importance. Plenty of worn-out cattle have been left along the trail for wolves to eat. I'll go back to the fort and offer the Mormon ten dollars for his cow. You can give me a horse for the money."

But before long Bordeaux came galloping back to the Brulé camp, to say that the Mormon had reported the theft of his cow to the soldiers and demanded that the "thieving redskins" be punished.

"The soldiers are bored with nothing to do," he panted. "They want some excitement. They talk of killing Indians for fun."

"What can I do?" Mat-to-i-o-way asked patiently. "The cow is eaten. I will give a good horse to take its place."

"*Sacré!* It is not enough," Bordeaux sputtered. "The soldiers are in a mood to start trouble."

Crazy Horse, who was among the crowd of Indians who gathered to hear what Bordeaux had to say, spoke up. "Brave Bear, one of the chiefs of my band, is the Lakota the soldiers call their Paper Chief. He is supposed to straighten out any trouble between the white men and the Indians. I am riding back to my camp now. I can tell him to go to the fort and talk to the soldier chief."

It made Crazy Horse feel quite important and a bit embarrassed when everyone turned to look at him.

"Good! Good!" Bordeaux said. "I was going to suggest sending for Brave Bear. After all, that's why the soldiers made him Paper Chief — to settle matters such as this." He seemed relieved to have the matter out of his hands.

So Crazy Horse rode back to the Oglala camp and told Brave Bear of the trouble in the Brulé village. Brave Bear put on his blue coat and the hat with the top cut out to make room for his eagle feathers and rode off to tell the white chief in charge of the fort that the killing of the Mormon cow was of no importance. The Brulés would pay a good horse for the animal.

Crazy Horse, wanting to be on hand when Brave Bear came, rode with his good friend He Dog back to the Brulé camp.

Soon Brave Bear came galloping. "The soldiers say that I must take Straight Foretop, who killed the cow, to the fort," he panted. "They want to arrest him."

At the word, "arrest," a murmur of horror rippled through the crowd of those who had gathered to listen. It meant to deprive a man of his freedom, to put him in a room with bars over the windows, to shut him away from light and air. The whites did this terrible thing even to their own people, but of course they were used to being cooped up within walls. Crazy Horse thought how dreadful it would be for any Indian, used to living out-of-doors, to be confined in the white man's prison.

"I will not go to the soldiers' fort," cried Straight Foretop, the visiting Miniconjou. "It is better to die fighting on the plains than to rot in the white man's jail."

A murmur of agreement arose from the bystanders. Indian etiquette forbade forcing a guest to do anything against his will, so Brave Bear had to ride back to the fort to tell the captain that the man who killed the cow was a Miniconjou — a guest in the Brulé camp so could not be brought in for arrest, but that the Brulés would pay five good horses for the one no-good cow.

Thinking that the matter was settled and that the Mormon was lucky to get five good horses in exchange for a cow too worn-out to travel, the Indians went about their affairs and soon most of the boys in camp were mixed up in a game of *Che-hoo-hoo*. They did not see Brave Bear ride back to camp to tell the Brulés to expect trouble.

The Indians, however, paid little heed to the Oglala chief. They thought he was inclined to be too swelled up with the importance of being the soldiers' Paper Chief. No doubt he was trying to make something out of nothing.

Crazy Horse and his friends were sitting on a rise of ground panting from their exertions in the wrestling game when Crazy Horse straightened up and pointed to the valley leading from the fort. There marched a double column of Blue Coats on foot. The one marching at the head of the column with his sword flashing in the sun must be the wild young man that Bordeaux said liked to talk about taking a "crack at the Sioux." As the soldiers came nearer the boys saw that they were dragging two wagon guns.

They raced pell-mell into camp, yelling, "The soldiers are coming! The soldiers are coming! With wagon guns!"

At once the older boys were sent to bring in the pony herds, to be ready if there was fighting to be done. Still the Brulés did not get very excited. Perhaps the soldiers had come to get the horses promised in payment for the cow. But why the wagon guns? Crazy Horse and He Dog hurried to the lodge where Straight Foretop was visiting. If the soldiers were going to arrest him, the boys wanted to see how such a thing was done.

Straight Foretop sat cross-legged on a buffalo robe, fanning himself with an eagle's wing. He seemed not much concerned with all of the excitement he was stirring up. The boys peered in at him, but at his unfriendly frown they dropped the flap of the tepee and backed away.

The soldiers were coming over the hill now. It was a pretty sight to see them marching in a line.

A tense atmosphere of waiting — silent waiting settled over the Brulé camp. Not even a dog barked. The women and children had gone into the tepees. The warriors stood beside their lodges with their bows in hand, but no one fitted arrow to bow.

Crazy Horse and He Dog stood motionless beside the lodge in which Straight Foretop sat fanning himself. On, on the Blue Coats came, stepping briskly. Their chief, Grattan, snapped out some order and they stopped walking and stood in a line.

Crazy Horse was fascinated. Never had he seen anything like this — many men walking in a straight line each with foot uplifted at the same time. Never had he seen grown men do things at the order of some one man. It was somewhat like a dance — but surely this was no dance. Now the soldiers all stood stiff and motionless with their faces pointed toward the camp.

Within Crazy Horse's range of vision there was only one flash of motion. That was Wyuse, the half-breed who served as interpreter at the fort. He was riding his horse up and down before the Indian village, slapping his mouth with his hand to make the Indian war whoops.

"He has had some of the white man's fire water," He Dog whispered.

Grattan, their chief, said something to Wyuse in his snapping tone.

"I will have you all killed," Wyuse yelled to the Indian camp. "I will eat your hearts before sundown."

Brave Bear came from his lodge, holding out his hands to show that they were empty, and walked slowly toward the white chief, Grattan.

"Bring out your thieving Miniconjou," Wyuse yelled.

Straight Foretop pushed aside the flaps of the tepee. "Stand back," he said to the Brulés. "I will never give myself up to be taken to the soldiers' prison. Let them kill me here on the plains. But stand out of the way, my friends. This is between me and the Blue Coats."

Crazy Horse and He Dog looked at each other and nodded their heads over the Miniconjou's bravery.

Then Grattan's arm came up and he shouted an order. Crazy Horse saw fire and smoke flower from the guns of the soldiers. Brave Bear ran up and down between the line of soldiers and his people.

"Do not let your arrows fly! Do not shoot the Blue Coats!" he begged the Brulés.

"Do not kill my helpless people!" he begged the Blue Coats.

Again the soldiers' rifles blazed and at the same time the two wagon guns boomed, tearing away the tops of tepees. Crazy Horse saw Brave Bear put his arms across his belly, then saw the blood gush over his arms and down his scrawny legs. The Paper Chief took two wobbly steps toward his tepee, then fell face forward. The women, peering between the flaps of their tepees, set up a mourning cry. Several of the older men rushed forward to carry the wounded Indian chief to his lodge.

Now the air was full of flying arrows and the sound of rifle fire. Screaming women and children ran in every direction. When he saw the old chief fall, a wave of horror and rage swept through Crazy Horse. He raised his own bow and fired at the Blue Coats. Now Grattan and all of the men near the wagon guns lay on the ground. The soldiers who had been at the edge of the camp were running up the road, pursued by the howling Brulés, some on horseback and some afoot.

It was over in a short time. Not one of the twenty-nine soldiers was left alive. The warriors were scalping and gashing the bodies of the slain soldiers. The smell of blood and gun smoke lay heavy on the air. Crazy Horse was sick in his stomach and was afraid that he was going to disgrace himself before his friend.

He Dog ran toward one of the bodies and struck it with his hand. "I, the brave He Dog, do count coup on the enemy," he yelled.

Crazy Horse followed his example and struck one of the bodies, crying, "I, Crazy Horse, do count coup on the

enemy." But he knew that his voice was thin and no feeling of triumph followed his act.

The two boys got on their horses and rode toward the Oglala camp. No talk passed between them. The horror of what they had seen was still too fresh in their minds. It had all happened so fast it seemed unreal. It was like a nightmare.

So that was what white men were like! Crazy Horse thought. He had been told that they were so powerful. So strong. But would men whose medicine was strong and powerful come and attempt to wipe out a peaceful Indian village merely for one worn-out cow? His chin sank on his breast as he jogged along trying to work out this confusing puzzle.

A great weariness weighed upon him. What was it all about — the coming of the whites and their strange actions? What would it mean to his people?

He was only twelve snows old, but he knew that in those terrible moments back there in the blood-soaked Brulé village he had left his boyhood behind him forever.

WHAT
WILL
HAPPEN
NEXT?

━━━━━━━ 6

He Dog prodded Crazy Horse from the deep reverie into which the sight of the massacre had plunged him.

"*Yekiya wo!* Let us hurry!" he cried. "We have important news to carry back to our people." His heels pounded the ribs of his pony.

Crazy Horse likewise urged Strongheart to a gallop. As they approached the Oglala village they gave the mourning cry, "Ey-ee!" to let the people know that they were bringing sad news.

The Indians poured from their tepees and clustered around the two boys on their ponies. They both talked at once, words spilling out on top of each other.

"Ey-ee! Ey-ee!" the keening sound broke from the women's throats at the news that their chief, Brave Bear, was so badly wounded.

The boys told of how brave he had been, walking straight

toward the soldiers' wagon guns, without so much as a bow
and arrow in his hand. He had asked them not to fire upon
his people — and had said that the matter of the cow could
be straightened out. Hearing these things, the Oglalas were
sorry that they had ever ridiculed the Paper Chief because
of the way he strutted about in the blue coat. Yes, their
chief had been very brave — and maybe had given his life
in an attempt to save his Brulé friends.

Almost before Crazy Horse and He Dog finished talking,
warriors were leaping on horses and riding toward Bordeaux's stone house to which their wounded chief had been
taken.

Crazy Horse gave his friend a meaningful look. Without
speaking each knew what was in the other's mind, and they
set out to follow the warriors. Having witnessed the beginning of such an important and exciting event, they did
not intend to miss what might follow.

Already a crowd seethed around Jim Bordeaux's place —
Brulés, Miniconjous, Oglalas — even a few Sans Arcs —
Lakotas all, who had been camped around the fort, drawn
there by the promise of gifts from the Great White Father
in Washington. There was a muttering noise, as of distant
roaring waters — a sound made by angry voices. The boys
hobbled their horses in order to get nearer to the core of
the crowd. Elbowing their way they squirmed through to
where Jim Bordeaux stood with his back against the door
of his trading house, talking, pleading with the chiefs. He
rubbed his fat hands together in distress. The sweat
streamed down his round face.

"Stay away from the fort, I beg of you," he cried. "*Sacré!*
Do not kill white men because of what a handful of foolish
ones did. You have already got your revenge — not a man
of Grattan's command left alive. The White Father will

likely forgive you if you do not add to what you have already done."

The angry roar from the wild young warriors grew louder at the trader's words.

"Do not try to storm the stone walls and the big guns of the Blue Coats at the fort," Man-Afraid-of-His-Horses cautioned the wild ones.

"There are only as many whites at the fort as we have fingers on two hands," the words rippled through the crowd.

A shiver went up Crazy Horse's spine at this news. He could imagine in what terror that handful of whites huddled within their stone fort waiting for news of the men who had gone forth to wipe out the Brulé village.

"Night fighting is not good," Hump told his warriors.

A murmur of agreement went through the crowd at this leader's sensible words. A fat moon rode the skies. All Oglalas knew that it was bad luck to fight by moonlight, and that any night fighting was bad. The people had been so wrought up that they had for a time forgotten that Oglala medicine was not good for night battles.

"We will wait for sunrise," the young men agreed sullenly.

Still the angry talk continued while the crowd seethed about the place. The fort should be attacked. All whites coming over the Holy Road should be killed. Even the traders, Bordeaux and those down the Platte, the American Fur Company, should be wiped out.

All night long this went on and Bordeaux continued to talk and then to bribe. He began giving away his goods — ropes of tobacco, hard bread, beads, vermilion, blankets, rolls of cloth. Two barrels of the sweet stuff called molasses were rolled out and the tops knocked off. Crazy Horse and

He Dog pushed their way to one of the barrels and dipped their fingers into the thick sticky substance. At first they touched their tongues to fingers gingerly, but after a taste, they dipped and licked greedily until they were shoved away.

At last Bordeaux's shelves were bare. He had nothing else to give. By the time the east grew pink, his face was haggard and drawn. All that he could do was to spread his hands helplessly and say again and again, until his voice croaked, "Wait! Wait!"

It was the Paper Chief's own people whose words threw the weight of caution to the wild young warriors, who were, after all, wearied by milling around all night.

"Brave Bear is not dead yet," they cried. "He still breathes. We had best wait to see whether or not he dies before we take further action."

Nearly everyone was ready now to agree with this sensible suggestion. Already some of the weary ones were straggling off to their sleeping robes. The edge of the excitement that had kept them awake all night dulled with the coming of daylight.

Crazy Horse and He Dog yawned in each other's faces and stumbled wearily to get their horses. They saw a stirring about the lodge to which the wounded chief had been taken after Jim Bordeaux had dressed his wounds. They rode over. Six strong Oglalas came from the lodge carrying their chief on a buffalo robe sling. His wife followed, softly keening her sorrow and carrying his blue coat and his soldier hat. The two boys joined the crowd which followed the litter.

Brave Bear's eyes were closed and his face was drawn with pain. Now and then he rolled his head and murmured words no one could understand.

"Do you think he will die?" He Dog whispered.

Crazy Horse shook his head. "He was wounded trying to save his people," he said. "Our medicine man can save him. If he should die. . . . "

He could not find words for what was in his heart. He shuddered. A sudden wave of hatred toward the whites swept through him. Its intensity surprised him. After all, he told himself reasonably after the wave had passed, it was not fair to blame all of them for the foolish act of one man, Grattan. Surely they were not all like that. There was Jim Bridger — the trapper who was a friend of the Indians. He spoke with the straight tongue and lived like the Indians and was respected by all of the Teton Sioux. There were other trappers like him — the little Kit Carson, for instance. No, it was not fair to blame all whites for the act of one.

Crazy Horse slept until the sun was past the middle. He found the people of the village moving restlessly about, gathering in small groups to talk, all the while watching anxiously for the mirror signals which flashed from the lookouts who were watching the Holy Road and the trail from the fort.

The messages were reassuring. No soldier trains were traveling over the Holy Road. No one had stirred from the fort, not even to bury their dead left at the now abandoned Brulé village.

On the way back to his tepee Crazy Horse came across his good friends, He Dog and young Hump. They beckoned to him mysteriously to follow. They made their way to the lodge of the wounded chief, and silently crept to the rear and cautiously lifted an edge and peered inside. The old man lay on his bed of buffalo robes. His face looked like a skull with yellow skin stretched over it. The hands which lay outside the robes looked like bird claws.

A stench came from the robes. There was no one in the tepee now save Running Horse, the medicine man, who had just arrived and was making a little square altar of earth close to the patient. As he worked he sang,

Come down healing
Come down healing
Holy man make well.

When the square of earth was ready they watched him kindle a small fire upon it and from a painted bag draw some herbs, which he threw upon the flames. Then he gave Brave Bear a piece of root to chew upon. He took a decorated rattle from a hide bag and began to sing and prance and shake his rattle to drive out the evil spirits which had seized the chief's body.

When the boys had first peered under the tepee the old chief had seemed to be asleep or in a stupor. Now he rolled his head and groaned. The medicine man ceased his din for a few moments while he threw more herbs on his little fire. Crazy Horse heard Brave Bear mumble, "Tell our young men not to fight. Tell them the white traders are our friends. The Oglalas must not kill for the evil one bad man did . . . " His voice trailed off and his skinny fingers clawed at the buffalo robe.

Crazy Horse stood up. It made his heart heavy to see the old man suffer. He hoped that the medicine man would be able quickly to chase away the evil left in the chief's body by the white man's bullets.

That night Crazy Horse was awakened by the shrill keening of the women. Immediately he knew what the sound meant: Brave Bear was dead. He sat up on his bed robes.

He heard the others in the tepee stir and the murmur of his father's and his stepmother's voices. He settled down again to wait for dawn, but not to sleep.

When dawn came, six warriors carried the body wrapped in Brave Bear's best robes to a scaffold erected in a grove of trees close to Shell River. The keening women followed the procession, their hair straggling, their arms gashed to show their grief. Now and then they stopped, picking up handfuls of dirt with which they rubbed their faces.

Crazy Horse and his friends straggled at the rear. The chief's wife led his favorite horse, decked out in war regalia. She carried his war bonnet in its embroidered bag and his bow and arrows. Other relatives carried food to sustain the old warrior on his journey to the Great Beyond.

The wailing increased as the procession stopped beneath a funeral scaffold. The body wrapped in its finery was placed on top. The white war horse was shot and its body left beneath. The food was placed on the ground. Brave Bear would enter the Happy Hunting Ground well equipped.

The crowd melted away. Crazy Horse slipped off from his friends to go and stand on a hilltop. He wanted to be alone to think about things. Deep depression weighed upon his spirits. What would happen now? Brave Bear's people had told the young warriors to wait and see whether their chief lived before they took any action against the whites. Now he was dead. Brave Bear himself had sent word for his people not to fight the whites. Almost with his last breath he had begged them not to be rash — to go off to their hunting grounds and forget the white men. But now his voice was stilled forever. What would happen?

GROWING
RIVALRY

∎∎∎∎∎∎∎∎ 7

THE BROAD LARAMIE PLAINS, where the Oglalas had moved, drowsed in the warm autumn sun. Crazy Horse, though, sensed the uneasiness of his people. The Brulés were camped close to the village of the Oglalas. There was a question in the minds of everyone. What would happen now? Would the soldiers come killing?

The dying Brave Bear had passed his power into the hands of Young-Man-Afraid-of-His-Horses, so called because he caused such dread in the hearts of his enemies that they feared even the sight of his horses. Crazy Horse watched with curiosity to see if his people would accept this leadership. He admired the tall, slim warrior whose bravery was unquestioned, but whose leadership had yet to be proved. In fact, the boy often puzzled over what quality made one man leader over others. What was the source of the power some men possessed that set them above the average? It was this power that he himself desired above anything on earth. Was it something, he wondered, with which the *Wakan Tanka* endowed some men, or was it a power a person could develop within himself?

He watched Man-Afraid carefully. What had Brave Bear seen in him to choose him as chief? The warrior, Hump, was fully as brave and distinguished. His pony herd was larger. The coups painted on his tepee were more plentiful. Often now the old men chiefs, Smoke, Whirlwind and Red Leaf, met in the lodge of Crazy Horse, the Holy Man, for councils. Man-Afraid was given the guest place at such meetings. Young Crazy Horse on his bed robes listened to the droning voices until sleep overpowered him. He hoped to hear Hump's name mentioned as a possible chief, but his hero was never talked of in this respect. One day when they were out hunting together the boy spoke of his resentment over the fact that Hump was not being talked of as chief.

"You are best fitted to be our leader," he said.

The warrior shook his head. "When you were about five snows old," he said, "the old men spoke of me as chief. But the *Wakan Tanka* did not put the desire for chieftainship in my heart. I have no wish for power."

"Does — does the wish for leadership — mean that the *Wakan Tanka* has made that person to be a great one among his people?" Crazy Horse asked hopefully.

The warrior glanced at him shrewdly as they rode side by side.

"It may be," he said quietly. "But I have known men with the lust for power who were not fit for leadership. To be great among our people a man must earn the honor. He must have bravery and wisdom. He should wish for power first because he wishes to serve his people. Then he should go often to speak alone with the Great Holy Mystery so that he will be guided to act right. You should be nearly ready for the Vision Quest."

"I have been thinking about it," Crazy Horse said. "I asked the *Wakan Tanka* for a vision the day you set me to fast, but nothing came."

"You were not ready," the warrior said. "You were but a boy then. I have been watching you. You are growing up fast. Soon you may ask your father, the Holy Man, to prepare you for the Vision Quest."

They jogged along in silence for a while, the boy busy with his thoughts. Suddenly he blurted, "If one yearns to be great among his people — how can he best prepare himself? What makes one man great — a leader, while most men stay like one of a herd?"

Hump shrugged. "You ask difficult questions, my son. I have no answer. I can teach you how to be a warrior. But the secret of greatness I do not know myself. That is something you must ask the Great Holy Mystery."

The question would not answer itself. Red Cloud was prominent among the Oglala, and it was easy for Crazy Horse to understand why this was so. He was a brave warrior and his coups were many. There was a dash about him that made people look his way when he rode or walked through the village with his swinging stride. And when he rose to tell of his coups beside the campfires, there was a ring to his deep voice and his words were strong and good and sent shivers up and down the spines of his listeners.

Man-Afraid was equally brave, but he did not have the gift of words that Red Cloud possessed. There was, however, a quiet air of confidence about Man-Afraid, and strength emanated from him as heat from the sun. He did not deck himself out in feathers and beaded robes the way

Red Cloud did, but wore a blue trader's blanket and went
about the village to see what his people needed, giving a
pony or meat to the poor and not making much noise about
what he did.

Crazy Horse liked his quiet way and tried to copy Man-
Afraid's air of confidence and strength. Crazy Horse decided that his own rival, No Water, was more like Red
Cloud. He also had a dashing air which caught attention,
and his words in the mock councils the boys held were
strong and many, whereas Crazy Horse could only say
quickly what he had to say, then sit down. Nevertheless, he
noticed that lately some of the boys seemed to be looking to
him for leadership, even though he was not so quick at
pushing himself forward as was No Water.

The uneasiness which had lain over the Lakota camp
eased when the moon changed from fat to a thin crescent,
then fat again with no soldier lines marching from the fort
or up the Holy Road. Brave Bear had told his people not
to attack the white men, but the wild young relatives of the
slain chief could not let matters rest. This was, of course,
one of those things that must be done.

Crazy Horse, He Dog and young Hump together watched
the young men, Long Chin, Spotted Tail, Red Leaf, Conquering Bear and Bull Bear in war paint and regalia ride
solemnly through the village, singing their war songs. Crazy
Horse was sick with longing for the time when he should
be such a warrior, stared at and admired by all of the
people. He and his friends were beside the campfire when
the brave warriors returned to tell of how they had waited
by the Holy Road until a wagon box appeared — what the
white men called the mail coach. They had slain the driver
and two men who rode cooped inside and had taken their

scalps. Also they had three good horses and some green paper and silver pieces taken from a strong box.

"Hau!" The coups were good, everyone agreed. Nothing like this had been done before.

After every angle of the exploit of the young warriors had been discussed, Man-Afraid rose to his feet and said, "Now that Brave Bear's death has been avenged, it will not be good to stay about the fort of the white men. Bad things have come to our people from being too close to the whites. Let us go to our home — the land the *Wakan Tanka* made for the use of his red children. There we will make our winter meat — gain new strength from the Holy Mystery and forget the bad things that have come from the white men."

"Hau!" the murmur of agreement rose from the throats of the people. A wave of relief rippled through the crowd at this decision. The uneasiness that had held them ever since the Grattan trouble dropped from them like a shed blanket.

Crazy Horse was happy as the Oglalas rode toward their beloved *Pa Sapa* — Black Hills. This was sacred ground to them — a gift from the *Wakan Tanka* — a place which provided every need: all sorts of game, lodge poles, rocks for their utensils, roots, leaves and fruit for medicine, food and dyes. But most important, because of its sacredness, it was a place where the Sioux renewed themselves spiritually.

Altogether it was the most pleasant winter in the memory of Crazy Horse, with many hunts with the warrior Hump and his son, with buffalo-rib sled races down the icy hills, with skating on wooden strips lashed to their feet, with ice pulls in which two sides tugged at a rawhide rope, yelling, laughing, falling in piles.

There was only one thing to mar the pleasure of the

winter for Crazy Horse. Some of his friends including young Hump and He Dog had been invited to join the Fox Warrior Society, but he had been ignored. No Water was already a member and put on an air of superiority over the coveted honor.

Again the old feeling of being alone made Crazy Horse miserable.

But now the sun was coming nearer, warming the earth, melting the snow and ice, bringing out a froth of leaves on the trees and shrubs, making the grass green.

At this time a restlessness came over the people again. They remembered the good things of the white man's stores. The women grumbled about having no beads ready to sew for embroidery; no cloth already made that did not have to be tanned; none of the sweet stuff the white men called molasses. The men spoke of the need of knives, of signal mirrors, of blankets, of guns with powder and balls to shoot in them.

So down the tepees came. Goods were piled on travois and the Oglalas and Brulé friends once again set their faces toward the white man's fort on the Platte.

"WHERE
ARE
MY
PEOPLE?"
■■■■■■■ 8

S EVERAL SLEEPS LATER Crazy Horse dropped behind the procession of Indians on the move while they went on to set up their camps. He sat astride Strongheart, alone atop a hill staring in amazement at a long line of white-topped wagons swaying over the road to Fort Laramie. The country of the whites must surely be deserted, he thought, with so many going toward the setting sun and never returning. He saw wagons clustered around the fort while a great circle of country was grazed bare by the many oxen and cattle.

Slowly he rode to where his people were busy setting up their camps beyond the grazed-off circle so that there would be grass for their ponies.

The grass was poor; there was no hunting so close to the fort. The whites with their creaking wagons, their lowing oxen and shrill yelling had driven the game far from the trail. Man-Afraid's Oglalas broke camp after a few sleeps and moved north of the fort for better hunting, close to the Brulé camp of Little Thunder. Almost at once conflict broke out in the village. There were those who had wanted to remain close to the fort because of the good things the white man had to give; others said the old way of the Indians was better.

The trouble grew so bad that some of the families moved back close to the Holy Road and the fort. Crazy Horse was glad that his father decided to remain here near the fascinating region of the Bad Lands, where there was good hunting and fishing, herds of wild horses to chase and catch, and interesting country where Indian boys could hide and play at battles. He was thirteen snows old — almost a man. He must waste no time in preparing himself to be a warrior, and he had no liking for the white man's ways.

Life here was very pleasant. He had struck up a firm friendship with Crow Feather, a Brulé boy about his own age. The two became inseparable companions. He was training Warrior, his red stallion which he had caught in the Great Sandhills, to be a war pony and the Brulé friend was a big help. Riding Strongheart, he would come yelling and charging with his lance. Crazy Horse, mounted upon Warrior, was teaching him to respond instantly to signals of knee, hand and voice — to turn swiftly as a mirror flash — to charge, wheel and pull up on haunches. It was fine training for both horses as well as for the boy warriors.

Then often, choosing sides, groups of boys would ride off for the Bad Lands for mock battles. Crazy Horse had his own small following now, with No Water usually the "war chief" of the opposite side.

Crazy Horse often thought of the manner in which the soldiers drilled outside the walls of the fort, each man's feet

rising and falling in time. He had been amazed to see them fight in a unit during the Grattan affair, under the orders of their chief instead of individually as the Indians did.

"It might be a good way to do battle," he told some of his comrades one day when they were choosing sides.

"*Waugh!*" scoffed No Water. "Our Sioux wiped out Grattan's soldiers to a man. Why do you say that is a good way to fight?"

Young Hump and others agreed with No Water and even Crazy Horse's few followers had no liking for this manner of fighting. Everyone knew that a warrior fought for individual honors.

So Crazy Horse had to let his followers fight in their own fashion. He was not strong enough among them to impose his will on theirs. But the old way of fighting was fun, he had to admit, and he gloried in his own coups to recount as he and his comrades huddled about their campfires in the evening.

The summer sped by. It was the Moon of Plums Turning Ripe when a new white chief came to take charge of the fort. News runners hurried to the Oglala camp telling that he was white-headed and with hair on his face. Every day he took his Blue Coats outside the walls of the fort and had them do the show-off marching and drilling in lines while he barked orders.

Soon after the white chief sent word that all friendly Indians must immediately move south of the Platte River.

The Oglalas looked at each other in dismay over this order. This country was theirs. For years they had roamed and hunted and lived where they pleased. Why should they now take orders from the white chief of the fort? The Oglalas and Brulés held a council in the lodge of Crazy Horse, the Holy Man.

"I will stay here where I like the country, where there is game for my people," Little Thunder said. "We do not wish to be beggar Indians — Loafers-Around-the-Fort. The old ways of the Sioux are good ways."

"But we should go in and hold council with the white chief," Man-Afraid advised. "They have many thunder sticks and wagon guns. No doubt the Great White Father is angry with Brave Bear's young men who killed the men on the box wagon."

Young Crazy Horse listening from his bed robes thought this poor advice. Everyone knew that the death of Brave Bear had to be avenged. That was the Sioux custom. The relatives of the old chief would have been disgraced had they not followed this custom.

The old men and the warrior chiefs powwowed until the night grew gray with the dawn, but young Crazy Horse had long ago drifted into slumber.

Man-Afraid, Old Smoke, Little Thunder and some of the others rode off to Bordeaux's house to have a talk with the white soldier chief. He told them that the White Father was very angry over the killing of the men on the box wagon and that he knew which warriors had done this thing. That they, the guilty ones, should remain north of the Platte, but that all of the friendly Sioux must come south of the Platte where they would be treated well and given many presents.

When the Oglalas and Brulés received this news they broke into little bands and started moving south.

"I will not go," Little Thunder said stubbornly. "Why should we go to the soldiers' fort? There is no game. No grass. We would have to live by the white man's laws which we do not understand. The soldiers know that my people are friendly — but we do not care for the white man's gifts.

There is good grass, good water, good hunting on the Blue Water. Tell the white chief he can find me here any time he comes looking."

Most of the Oglalas moved south, but a few remained with Little Thunder's camp. Among them were Crazy Horse's family.

"The white man's ways are not good for the Indian," the holy man said. "Only evil comes to our people who take his gifts and adopt his ways."

The families of He Dog and No Water were among those who moved south. The warrior Hump remained on the Blue Water with Little Thunder. Crazy Horse was happy that he was not to be separated from his new friend, Crow Feather. Never had he known such completeness of living and of thinking as when they were together.

■■■■■■■■■■

THE
VISION
QUEST

■■■■■■■■ 9

T HE HOT, BREATHLESS DAYS drifted by. Every day there were swimming contests, for this was the most pleasant of all sports in summer. But Hump did not allow his adopted son to play all of the time. Every day he must practice his skills. Every day he must practice shooting the bow and arrow and throwing the lance and riding.

"Troubled times are ahead for our people," Hump said one day. "We must have leaders wise and skillful."

His words made it seem as if a cloud had crossed the sun.

Some days later the warrior Hump said to Crazy Horse, "It is time you were training for the Vision Quest."

The boy caught his breath. He had, of course, known that this ordeal was before him — had hoped for it; but it had been one of those things that lay in the dim future. It pleased him that his teacher thought him ready for this experience, for it was one of the things that lay on the threshold of young manhood. He was nearly fourteen snows old. He had grown much taller since the last summer, but he was still slight of build. This lazy summer he had been happy in the companionship of Crow Feather and for the first time had not been so plagued by self-doubts and vague discontents. Did Hump's statement that he was ready for the Vision Quest mean that his boyhood was actually nearly over?

"Will you make me ready for the Quest?" he asked his friend.

Hump shook his head. "No, that is for your father, the Holy Man, to do," he said.

So Crazy Horse went to his father and asked to be prepared.

His father nodded. "I have been waiting for you to come to me," he said. "It is time."

So for a while the boy gave up all games and contests, to remain with his father in seclusion while the old man talked to him quietly of the holy things of the Sioux. He gave him a pipe with a red bowl and a carved handle and a finely embroidered bag of otterskin in which to keep it.

"This is the holy pipe of our people," he said, tamping down a mixture of leaves and bark, called *kinnikinnick,* and sweet sage in the bowl. He lighted it with a stick from the fire. He offered the pipe to the heavens, the earth and the four directions from whence came all good things. After a few puffs he handed it to the boy who also offered it to the six directions and took a few solemn puffs.

"This pipe," his father said, "was given to the Lakotas many years ago by the Sun Woman. It is holy among our people, for its smoke joins us to the *Wakan Tanka.* Every puff sent up in prayer reaches the Great Mystery above. That is why the pipe is used in our ceremonies, in sacred dances and in councils. Always guard this pipe and keep it holy for it is the symbol of the *Wakan Tanka*."

Often the father and son strolled away from camp to sit on some lonely hillside while the holy man talked quietly of sacred things in order that his son's mind would not dwell on food or games or things of the flesh but would become attuned to spiritual matters so that he would be ready to commune with the Great Holy Mystery.

"The *Wakan Tanka*," the older Crazy Horse said, "is the maker of the earth and all upon it. He breathed life into all things and set the sun in the sky to provide warmth and light for our people. We cannot breathe, we cannot look at anything on earth without putting ourselves in touch with the *Wakan Tanka*, for He is everywhere — even in the air we breathe."

These things Crazy Horse had realized in a vague way, but his father's words made the idea clearer in his mind.

"Will the Holy Mystery come to me in a vision?" the boy asked.

"I cannot say," his father replied. "Everyone seeks the vision and hopes for it. But it is granted to only a few. Those who have a service to perform for the people receive it — or those who are singled out for greatness."

Thoughts of his old ambitions came back to Crazy Horse. He had imagined himself doing great and brave things that caused all of his people to marvel. He had thought himself becoming great among the Lakotas. Now soon he would know if the *Wakan Tanka* had set him apart for greatness, or if he should content himself with remaining in the shadowy background of the crowd.

"I am ready for the long fast," Crazy Horse said, finally.

"*Hau*," his father agreed. "You are ready."

He led his son to the sweat bath lodge. Crazy Horse

seated himself cross-legged on a robe inside while his father
built a small fire of sweet sage in the center of the lodge.
His mother, meanwhile, built a fire outside and heated rocks
which were thrust inside, then water was poured over them,
making a cloud of steam. When he was covered with
perspiration, Crazy Horse ran outside and dived into the
stream. Now he was purified for the fast.

Following his father who carried a buffalo robe and skull
and his pipe, they went to a lonely hilltop where already a
small hide tepee had been erected over four poles, as four
was the sacred number of the Sioux. The old man made a
square altar before the tepee. This he covered with sage
and placed upon it the sacred buffalo skull facing the east.
He filled the pipe with sage, lighted it and after the six
directions ceremony, handed it to the boy.

"Keep your mind holy," he said. He looked at his son
for a long moment as if wishing to say more — perhaps to
give him greater strength and comfort. But now there was
nothing more he could do. For the first time in his life the
boy must face powerful, mysterious forces. And no one on
earth could help him.

His father turned and walked down the hill leaving his
son alone to fast and pray for four days and nights, or until
the vision came.

As he saw his father go down the hill Crazy Horse had an
impulse to cry out — to beg him to wait — not to leave him
alone. But he conquered the moment of panic and terror
and stood motionless and silent, watching until his father
was out of sight.

He looked about, feeling as if he were the only living
thing in this whole vast world. Then he remembered the
pipe in his hand. He put it to his mouth and puffed,
through its ascending smoke sending up his prayers to the

Wakan Tanka. He stood before the little shelter as he
smoked, facing the sun and as it moved he turned, following
its course.

"Make me great, *Wakan Tanka*," he prayed. "Grant me
a vision of guidance. Send a messenger to show me the
way."

He concentrated on his prayers, his smoking and staring
at the sun until a sense of exhilaration took hold of him.
This was the most important experience of his life. He
felt lifted above all his people.

But finally his muscles began to ache; his sight was
blurred. And when the sun dipped beyond the edge of the
world his spirits sank with it, leaving him chilled and de-
pressed. How alone he was! He was wrapped around with
solitude. It was inside of him. Everywhere. And it would
be eternal. He must walk forevermore alone — himself
against the world. No one could help him. How small and
insignificant he was. How absurd of him to feel that he
could ever become great — or that the Great Holy Mystery
would notice him.

Now as darkness crept over the world — as the sense of
this vast solitude and his own insignificance penetrated to
his innermost being, he felt that he could not endure it.
He must run away. But where? How could one run away
from what was inside himself?

He crossed his arms over his chest as if to hug himself —
to bring some warmth to his body. Then he crept into the
tepee, finding a bit of comfort in its shelter. He knew that
evil spirits roamed the world after the sun was hid, and
that wild animals were on the prowl, but they were not so
fearsome as this terrifying aloneness.

Now his stomach cramped with hunger and his mouth
and throat were parched, but at last he slept fitfully.

The second day dragged like a wounded animal. With each creeping hour his bodily discomforts increased. All day long he stood facing the sun, sending up his prayers for the vision and striving to keep his mind from the torments of hunger and thirst — and his terrible aloneness. The third day he was weak and so dizzy when he faced the sun that it dipped and whirled crazily. But his mind was light — seemed partly detached from himself. But still the vision did not come. The sun passed the middle and crawled again to the edge of the world.

Crazy Horse stretched forth his hands. "The vision, *Wakan Tanka!* The vision!" he pleaded.

Soon it would be dark. His father had told him that if the Vision did not come by nightfall of the fourth day, he need not expect it. Now it seemed to him that he could not go on living if the vision were not granted. Hunger and thirst were forgotten as his whole being went out in his desire for the message.

A moment ago the sun had been shining bright. Now the world suddenly became dark as a giant crash of thunder shook the universe, leaving round black and blue marks on his chest. He saw these marks when jagged lightning split the sky, casting eerie bluish light over the world and leaving its jagged outline on his cheek. By that light he saw the splendid white stallion come from the clouds. Without knowing how it happened, he was on the stallion's back, at the head of a great crowd of people. Another giant crack of thunder, then the skies split wide open with dazzling light and he saw before him many people lying on the ground as though dead. Still the stallion he was on galloped at the head of the throng. All the while these things were happening, Crazy Horse was sharply aware of a red hawk circling above his head with a round, blue stone in its beak.

Once again the heavens split open and in that brief moment Crazy Horse understood the meaning of all things. Never would he be quite the same again. Then suddenly the blackness came.

A small red disk of sun was peeping over the edge of the world — but it was in the east, not the west. Crazy Horse sat up blinking. Then he remembered. The vision had come to him just at sundown. Now it was morning. He struggled to his feet, holding out his hand to the sun, while his heart poured out wordless thanks to the Great Holy Mystery for the vision. He was set apart. He had work to do leading his people. A spirit of exaltation still held him, putting strength into his limp legs. He remembered the vision as clearly as if it were happening again. Once more the words of the red hawk rang out, "When you need strength — guidance from the Holy One, go away by yourself. Only by being alone can one understand the meaning of things."

He chanced to look at the ground and there at his feet lay a round, blue stone. The one which the hawk had carried in its mouth! Slowly he stooped and picked it up and turned it over and over in his hand.

He walked slowly down the hillside. He must go to his father and tell him of the vision and receive his interpretation. As he came closer to the valley of the Blue Water, where his people were camped he saw the strange cloud which hung over the place. Was this cloud and the heavy odor of smoke a part of his dream in which had appeared thunder and lightning?

He topped a little rise overlooking the village, then his heart leaped like a frightened thing, for there below lay no peaceful Indian village with the smoke of campfires twisting upward. Before him there was no living object —

only a ruined camp with burned tepees and bodies of his people lying all around.

Was this part of the vision? He stumbled forward slowly, staring down in horror at what he saw. No, this was certainly no vision from the *Wakan Tanka*. This was instead, evidence of the passage of evil forces — of the Blue Coats marching with thunder sticks and wagon guns. They had blasted a path of destruction through Little Thunder's village, leaving bodies of men, women and children strewing their trail.

As the reality of this horror swept over Crazy Horse he hurried through the destroyed village staring down into glassy eyes, turning over bodies to see who they were. Then a sudden cry strangled in his throat as he gazed into the twisted features of his dear friend, Crow Feather, and beside him lay his mother clasping the body of her baby in her arms.

Strange, hoarse cries rasped from Crazy Horse's throat. He ran fearfully toward the village of his own people, dreading what he expected to see. The Oglala village had been closer to the white man's fort. But now it was deserted. The tepees were left standing, but the people were gone. It, too, was a desecrated village with an air of death hovering about it, like the camp of Little Thunder, but without the slashed and blasted bodies and burned lodges.

A cry which seemed to wrench itself from the very core of his being came from his lips, "Where are my people? Oh, where are they?"

With stunned spirit and glazed eyes he stumbled forward.

THE
GREAT
GATHERING 10

DAZED, CRAZY HORSE roamed about the camp looking for he knew not what. His people were gone. He realized that there was no use looking for them here, yet in desperation he peered into each empty tepee.

He was so stunned that for a time he forgot that he was weak from hunger. Beyond the tepees Blue Water Creek rippled placidly. The sight and sound of the running water caught his whole attention. Thirst! That was it. He ran to the stream, threw himself on his stomach to drink in long, greedy gulps. Then he wandered back to the deserted camp for more aimless searching. He found a hide bag of *wasna* and stuffed hunks of it into his mouth.

As the morning passed he gradually gathered strength. He searched each tepee — turned over every dead body but his own people were not among them. Perhaps, then, they were still alive. He began searching for tracks of fleeing

Indians and found them going in every direction. It was evident that the Oglalas had scattered in panic. He followed the most prominent trail, finding along the way discarded equipment, broken travois and other evidence of haste.

The food he had eaten and his anxiety strengthened his limbs. Setting out at a dog trot, he came at last to a place where several trails joined showing him that his scattered people were gathering again. But they were turning back toward the hated fort! What could they be thinking of? As the remembrance of what he had seen back there on the Blue Water flooded his mind with terrible pictures, hatred for the whites boiled into his heart — made his stomach tighten into a hard core. They had brought nothing but evil — nothing but trouble to his people. He would hate them every day of his life.

He followed the trail until it became too dark to see, then he looked about for a place to sleep, found a cave close by and crept into it to sleep fitfully until dawn.

At daylight he picked up the trail again. The night's rest in the warm cave had restored his clear thinking, but a gnawing ache in his heart tormented him. Crow Feather, the dearest friend he ever had, was gone forever. It was as if a part of himself had been slain.

The vision he had experienced on the hillside took on meaning now. The *Wakan Tanka* had work for him to do. Through *Itun-hota*, the red hawk, he had sent the message. Always he had longed for power, but it had been a selfish desire. Now he felt that the power he had longed for was in him — but it was given him for a purpose. He must use it to serve his people. He must save them from the evil forces let loose upon them by the coming of the white men. As he walked he felt that the burdens of the entire Sioux nation rested on his shoulders, but he felt strong enough to bear them.

It was not until his shadow was long that Crazy Horse came to the village of his people, where they had been driven near the white man's fort.

To all outward appearance the village was quiet and mournful, but underneath it seethed with suppressed fury. In his father's tepee Crazy Horse heard the story of what had happened on the Blue Water. The sun was still low in the east when the walking soldiers had come marching. Frightened, some of the women started pulling down the tepees and moving with their children to the hills to the north.

"We are peaceful people!" Little Thunder told his Brulé. "Why should we run like scared dogs?"

With Spotted Tail and Iron Shell holding white flags, he sent his old men out to the near-by hillside to powwow with the soldier chief called Harney. While the chiefs smoked their pipes and counseled with the general, more walking soldiers with wagon guns made a large circle around the camp.

Young Crazy Horse's features grew hard as he listened to his father tell the story. The holy man, usually a calm, quiet man, paced back and forth and waved his arms as he talked.

Spotted Tail had come back to camp to report to Little Thunder. "Those who killed Grattan as well as those who attacked the wagon box must be given up. The soldier chief says they must come to him," he announced.

"Who can point out which man killed the one they call Grattan?" Little Thunder answered calmly. "When the Blue Coats fired, we all fought as men should to protect their village."

When Spotted Tail returned to give Little Thunder's message to the soldier chief, Harney, the Blue Coats were already lined up for battle. The soldiers did not wait to hear what word Little Thunder had sent; the thunder sticks blazed; the wagon guns blasted through the village mowing down the Brulé.

"Our people fell down dead. All over the ground. In front of their tepees."

The older Crazy Horse sank to the ground, spent from the telling of the terrible events. He put his head in his hands and moaned, "Over one hundred of our people taken prisoner. And almost as many slain."

"I know!" his son cried. "I saw what happened. All of our good people lying on the ground, dead. My good friend, Crow Feather, too!"

A lump came in his throat, choking off the words. Biting his lips hard, he turned his face away from his father.

"Little Thunder was badly hurt," his father went on, pretending not to see the distorted muscles of his son's face. "So was our brave Man-Afraid. His deeds that bad day will live long in our people's memories. Armed only with his lance, he saved a friend's life and killed as many Blue Coats as I have fingers on two hands."

There was a long silence as father and son thought of the terrible things which had happened.

"The white men took both of your horses," the holy man went on.

Young Crazy Horse had heard enough. He could not listen any longer. His heart was too heavy with sorrow for the loss of his friend for him to take in all of the details of what had happened to others. He left the tepee and wandered off alone into the hills.

Would he ever know happiness again, he wondered.

Never before had he felt a desire to kill. Now it was so strong in him that he raised clenched fists and shouted hoarsely, "I will kill! Kill! Kill! All my life I will kill white men. Until none is left on earth!"

The shadows were long when he stumbled back into camp. On the way he had passed a group of soldiers drilling outside the fort. As they marched they sang:

> *We did not make a blunder,*
> *We rubbed out Little Thunder*
> *And we sent him to the other*
> *   side of Jordan.*

Crazy Horse did not know what the words meant, but he caught the name Little Thunder and sensed that they had something to do with his people. When he got back to camp he told his father about the soldiers' song.

The holy man shook his head sadly. "They sing those words every day," he said. "One of the traders told us the meaning of the words. But they did not wipe out Little Thunder. He was wounded but is recovering in a secret camp."

"And what news of our people?" the boy asked. "The ones they hold inside the fort?"

"The white chief called Harney," the old man replied, "sent a messenger to say that they will be kept prisoner until those who attacked the mail wagon give themselves up."

"They will never do that!" Crazy Horse cried. "Spotted Tail is one of our bravest warriors. He will find a way. He is not the sort to rot in the white man's prison."

"Our chiefs have asked the young warriors to give themselves up for the good of all our people," the holy man said. "The white man chief promised to give us back our people they hold prisoner and they promise not to attack our camps if the warriors give themselves up."

"It is bad!" Crazy Horse said. "The Blue Coats will come killing again if those who attacked the box wagon do not go in. And there is no telling what they will do to those they hold prisoner. But how terrible for the young warriors who have to go in to be shut within walls!"

In a few days Spotted Tail, Long Chin, Red Leaf and Conquering Bear came down from their hiding place into camp dressed in their finest war garments. The air filled with the keening cries of the women as the warriors, chanting their death songs, marched through the village on their way to the soldier fort.

Crazy Horse's throat grew tight as he saw them go forth so bravely to sacrifice themselves for their people. What they were doing was far harder, far braver than going into battle. And for this deed they could count no coups.

The four young warriors who marched to the fort to surrender were not slain, as everyone had expected they would be. Two days later Crazy Horse and his people, angry and helpless, watched from a little hill outside the fort while Spotted Tail and his brave friends, their arms and legs bound in chains, were taken off in a wagon. What would be done to them? Where were they being taken? No one knew. And the Brulé women and children held captive within the fort were not released as the White Beard, Harney, had promised.

Muttering to each other the Oglalas and Brulés came down from the hill after the wagon was out of sight. Once this had been their land where they could do as they pleased. Now, even though they were not shut within walls, it was as if they were prisoners, with no one knowing what would happen to them next.

That night Crazy Horse got He Dog, young Hump,

Touch-the-Clouds and Charging Bear and they crept upon the soldiers' pony herd outside the fort — the herd in which were many of the Indians' horses taken from them on the Blue Water. Crazy Horse gave his shrill whistle. He heard a whinny and in a moment Strongheart nuzzled his shoulder. With a yell of triumph, Crazy Horse leaped to the animal's back, then with wild yells the boys stampeded the rest of the herd and drove it far away. The guards' rifles spat fire, but in the dark no one was hit. It was only a little thing but it would cause the soldiers much trouble. It was his first step in vengeance toward the whites and it gave Crazy Horse a satisfied feeling.

It seemed to him that the hatred aroused in his soul back there in the devastated camp of Little Thunder had hardened within him, making him strong. There was a new firmness in his step and in his manner and even No Water treated him with respect. His father noticed the change in him.

"You are different, my son," he said one evening as they sat eating meat. "Your face has lost the soft lines of boyhood. You are only fourteen snows old. Yet lately you seem like a man."

"*Hau!*" Crazy Horse agreed. He did not tell his father of his plans to have vengeance upon the whites — or even of his vision. He preferred to shut his thoughts inside of himself. But thinking and planning of the things he would do someday made him feel strength rise up within him. The *Wakan Tanka* had destined him for greatness — greatness he would win by fighting the whites. That was what his vision had meant. He did not need his father's interpretation.

Silently at night — although they hated traveling by dark, many groups of the Sioux were stealing away from their camps near the fort. Crazy Horse's people were among those who moved toward the Powder River country where they could find grass and game and freedom, away from the White Beard's rule. There they could live the way the Great Mystery intended his people to live. The Platte Valley had become the land of the whites; the Sioux could remain there only under the white man's laws, but the Powder River country was still virgin wilderness — a lovely land, blue, green and gold in summer. And over it loomed the Big Horn Mountains. Here there were forests, rivers, quiet lakes, grassy meadows of feed for the ponies — and game enough for all of the Plains Tribes. The tension eased from Crazy Horse's spirits as he gazed at the *Ah-sah-ta,* Big Horns, so named because they curved like the horns of the sheep which inhabited their rocky heights. Peace and happiness entered his soul. Here was his true Homeland. Here his people could live out their days, hunting, stealing horses, fighting Crows — unmolested by the white men. Life would be good once more.

After a quiet winter news runners came bearing the pipe summoning all of the numerous bands of Teton Sioux to a great powwow to be held at Bear Butte near the Black Hills country to decide what to do about the increasing invasion of the whites upon their lands. The word of the attack on the village of friendly Indians of Little Thunder had traveled like the stirring beat of war drums across the prairies. Never had any band of Teton Sioux suffered such a humiliating defeat; the entire camp taken, nearly one hundred dead, and women and children still held prisoner within the fortress gates; their brave young men taken away in irons!

At first Crazy Horse resented having the old trouble brought up again after its fever had subsided. Yet, in a

way it did his heart good to have his people on the move
again after the long winter. Although there had been the
usual sports and games and much hunting of fat game, yet
his heart had stirred with a restlessness for he knew not
what. It was as if he were past being a boy, but not yet
ready to be a man. He should be doing something of importance, but he did not know what it was. For five sleeps
they traveled. As he moved with his band toward the Bear
Butte country, much of the restlessness dropped from him.
It was as though he were riding toward the strange something he must do.

From all of the directions the numerous tribes of the
Lakotas came pouring in. Every night when they made
camp, new groups joined them. It was like many streams in
flood time flowing downward toward a lake. It was a wonderful sight when they were all gathered, their tepees
spreading in a huge circle. Crazy Horse galloped Strongheart from one camp to another and it made his heart glad
to see how strong his people were.

Often he with young Hump, He Dog and Touch-the-
Clouds squatted on the fringes of the meetings about the
central campfire where the chiefs talked of what should be

done about the whites. Crazy Horse was glad to see that the Oglala chief, Man-Afraid, was strong among the older chiefs. Red Cloud, too, was powerful in the meetings as he stood up in the firelight, tall and straight and spoke words wise and true. Spotted Tail, who had finally been turned loose by the soldiers, was there, too. But his power was gone. He had changed — his mind had become mixed up with white man's thoughts and no longer were his words strong in councils.

Red Cloud's voice rang out, "We are many as the buffaloes in the herds before the white men thinned them out," he waved his hands, taking in the great crowd gathered about the campfire. "We bowed too easily to the Blue Coats. We let them take our women and children to shut behind walls. Why did we not fight them until they ran like frightened antelope?"

"That is what we should do," Crazy Horse said to himself. "We are strong. We should band together and drive the whites from our land."

"Hau! Hau!" rose the chorus of agreement from the young warriors.

"We cannot fight them," came Spotted Tail's discouraging voice. "I have been among them. I have seen their strength. The White Father has many guns. Many men. We cannot fight them."

The crowd turned upon him with a hissing noise as of a snake about to strike.

"I know what I am talking about," he repeated. "They are too many."

"A warrior prefers to die fighting," Red Cloud spoke up.

Again the *"haus"* of agreement rose. Here, Crazy Horse thought, is the coming man of the Oglalas and a wave of envy swept through him. Red Cloud was the sort of hero he wished he could be — great in deeds and one the people listened to in councils. But he, Crazy Horse, did not possess the gift of words. Would he ever be great in deeds, he wondered? Would the prophecy of leadership he had received during the Vision Quest ever come true? Following that time his feeling that he was destined to do something great for his people had been strong, but the feeling had diminished with each moon.

It was a time of feasting, of visiting, of dancing and courtships and of powwows. It made all of the Sioux realize their strength to see the extent of their numbers, for this was the first time within the memories of any of them that a meeting of all of the western Lakota tribes had been held.

Crazy Horse marveled at the greatness of his people. His own band of Hunkpatilas was one of the seven bands of Oglalas; the Oglalas were one of the seven divisions of the Teton; and all of the Tetons were one of the seven great council fires of the Lakota nation. Their sacred number seven within the great sacred circle of seven. *Hau!* They were strong indeed. Why should they bow to the will of the whites?

The great council broke up with the people feeling their might. They would resist the whites. They would hold their lands — live the good life of their fathers.

HE
WILL
BE
GREAT
.... 11

AFTER THE GREAT COUNCIL the Lakotas traveled back to the Big Horns country. The whites were far away and the memory of their bad times with them dimmed as the moons passed with hunting and fishing and the good ways of Indian life. Gradually the dark cloud which had descended upon the spirit of Crazy Horse when he stared into his friend's glazed eyes on the Blue Water eased away and he could again be happy. The flaming hatred he held toward the whites died to embers. What had happened now seemed like a bad dream.

Yet there was still that strange restlessness in his heart. The feeling of strength which had come to him after the Vision Quest returned now and then, but the games and contests of the Oglala boys did not satisfy him now. He longed to test his strength in more manly occupations. One day he chose a small band of his followers: He Dog, young Hump, Touch-the-Clouds, Charging Bear, Spotted Elk and Crow King and led them off into the hills to talk of his plans. They had a difficult time eluding No Water, who was becoming jealous because some of the boys followed Crazy Horse. The older boy sought to belittle and hamper his rival in every way possible.

After their plans were carefully made the boys walked back to camp, parting company shortly before they arrived so that they would approach one at a time and from different directions. Acting very casually, they went to their respective tepees. Crazy Horse took down from a lodge pole the small hide medicine bag he had prepared some time before in accordance with his vision. It contained the dried body of a red hawk, the round blue sacred stone and some sweet sage, and his own war paints. He hung a bag of *wasna* from his belt. He filled his stomach with meat from the stew pot and, taking a rope and robe, and sack of well-ripened meat, he walked slowly and in an apparently aimless manner to the edge of the village.

Going over a slight rise that shut him off from sight of the camp, he broke into a run until he came to the boulder which was to be their meeting place. He sat behind this to wait until his companions appeared. They came, one at a time as had been planned. When they were all gathered, they set out toward the north, walking briskly. They walked until nightfall; then in a sheltered spot they lay on the ground to sleep. At sunrise they set out again. For three sleeps they traveled; then late one afternoon Crazy Horse pointed out a thin wisp of smoke twisting toward the sky.

They slackened their pace. Coming close to the top of

a hill they glided from bush to bush until they could peer down into the valley below in which nestled a Crow Indian village.

The boys looked at each other with grins of triumph, then settled down in a secluded spot to eat *wasna*. They must wait until long after the sun died. They stretched themselves out on the ground and after nightfall some of them slept, but not Crazy Horse. He was the leader of this expedition; his was the responsibility. He must not fail. This was to be the test of his new-found strength. It would prove, in part, if his vision were real or only a dream.

He twisted his hair in a knot on the front of his head, then took the body of the red hawk from his medicine bag and fastened it on the side of his head with sharp twigs. He tied the blue sacred stone back of his left ear with a piece of sinew. He drew the zigzag mark of lightning across his right cheek with yellow paint and made dots over his chest to represent thunder.

His preparations completed, he wakened his comrades and they set out, creeping through the bushes toward the Crow camp.

Pointing to a herd of horses, he said, "You take the ponies at the edge of the camp. I will go into the village itself. Move swiftly, quietly. If the Crows attack, run for the brush where we ate our *wasna*. Keep as many horses as possible. Remember, this expedition is to get horses, not coups."

On silent feet he ran into the heart of the village, tossing hunks of meat to the dogs to keep them from barking. The large painted lodge of the chief loomed in the middle of the village. Crazy Horse sped to it, and quickly cut the rope which tied a fine horse to a stake close to a tepee. The animal snorted as Crazy Horse fastened the rope around his

jaw. He became motionless for a moment, but no one stirred within the lodge. He cut another horse from beside the next tepee and yet another and another until he was leading four.

This was enough. It was foolish to take too many chances, endangering his comrades. *Hoye!* This was great! Stealing ponies right from under the noses of the Crows. And one of them a chief! Excitement rose in Crazy Horse's veins until he wanted to laugh aloud. Then a dog barked. It was the signal for pounding hoofs as the boys outside the village drove off the ponies they had rounded up.

"Hi-yi-yi!" came shrill yells from the lodges. Crazy Horse leaped upon the back of the chief's fine horse, still holding the ropes of the others and raced toward the brush. The moonlight shone on his comrades driving their stolen ponies.

Well Crazy Horse knew that the Crows would not dare attack them once they were barricaded behind the brush and fallen timber, for they had no way of knowing how strong his horse stealing band was.

The Crows fired a few futile arrows into the brush. The boys shot several in return; then the Crows retired to their village to await the coming of day, leaving several of their members to stand guard. But by daylight the Oglala boys were far away, riding lickety-split on the stolen ponies and driving the others.

That night a feast was held in their honor and Crazy Horse, as leader, was asked to stand up and tell about the exploit. He spoke modestly, wishing he had the tongue of Red Cloud, but when he sat down everyone spoke in praise of such daring boys.

"They will be great warriors," everyone said.

The quiet days passed quickly, but after the pony stealing

expedition, Crazy Horse was more restless than ever. After such a thrilling adventure, games and mock battles seemed tame to him.

So the winter the Lakota history man called The Snow of White Bear Holding passed, with nothing more exciting than the one horse stealing expedition against the Crows. And people soon stopped talking about that event. The rivalry between No Water and Crazy Horse raged stronger than ever now, for a number of boys had deserted No Water to become the followers of Crazy Horse. But since the horse stealing exploit was no longer big news to be talked about, some of them were returning to No Water, who still had a dash and confident air about him that Crazy Horse lacked.

The next summer there were only a few Oglalas who talked about returning to the soldiers' fort. Most of them had had enough of the white men and it was finally decided to remain near the Big Horns where the hunting was even better than in the Black Hills. Also, the Crows and Gros Ventres were close so that there could be occasional pony stealing raids and other forays for excitement and for gathering coups.

The summer sped by with nothing much beside the usual doings until some Brulé visitors one day brought in a white boy they had captured riding over the Holy Road. They said that every day two of these boys passed each other at full gallop. At the stations they would slide from their ponies, slip the flat saddle onto the back of a fresh mount which was held waiting for them, then speed away. It was very mysterious. The Brulés said these boys called themselves Pony Express riders. They had brought one into camp to see what it was that he carried that made him ride so fast.

The Oglalas pulled the boy from the saddle. He fought

like a warrior when they took the saddlebags and tried to
open them. They were shut tight with small metal pieces,
so they had to slit open the leather. The boy rider had to
be held fast by the arms to keep him from grabbing the bags
away. The Indians gave "Phaughs" of disgust when they
found the bags held only folded pieces of paper, of no interest or value whatsoever. Yet the boy rider, as soon as he was
released, went about with an angry expression picking up
the papers and stuffing them back into the cut bags.

"Let him go," Crazy Horse said. "He is brave. What he
carries is of no good to us. Just more strange notions of the
whites."

For the moment Crazy Horse had forgotten his one-time
hatred of all whites. The boy's bravery had aroused his admiration; he did not want such a brave one harmed. They
let him go.

Crazy Horse was sixteen snows old and seemed to be no
closer to his goal of becoming a great warrior than he was
when the ambition for greatness was first born in his heart.
The lifted-up feeling of the Vision Quest had remained
with him for some time, but it had gradually faded. Often
now he had doubts that he was destined for leadership —
for service to his people. Actually he was an unimportant
boy who had never even had a feast in his honor.

One day his friend young Hump brought him word that
his father was planning a raid against the Gros Ventres
who had become too daring in their horse stealing raids.

"It is time," Crazy Horse spoke calmly, trying to keep the
excitement from his voice. His friend's words had given
birth to an idea in his mind.

As soon as he was able he left his companions and hurried
to the warrior's lodge.

"I am going with you," he announced boldly.

A smile twitched at Hump's lips as he asked quietly, "You think you are ready to become a warrior?"

"I am ready," Crazy Horse said with such an air of quiet confidence that Hump looked at him shrewdly.

"*Hau!* You are ready," he agreed. "We are about to start. Get your things."

Crazy Horse hurried to his tepee for his bow and arrow, war club, medicine bag and paints. His trader's knife he always carried in its sheath fastened to his gee string.

The morning sun was just peeping over the edge of the world when he mounted Strongheart and hurried after the band of braves who were already setting forth. The leader at last gave the signal to stop. They dismounted behind a clump of bushes to prepare for battle. From beautifully decorated buckskin bags they took quill-embroidered shirts and moccasins, which they donned, then painted their faces.

Crazy Horse had no fancy bag nor war garments. All that he had was his medicine bag. He took out the body of the red hawk which he fastened to the side of his head. Then he drew the zigzag lightning mark on one cheek and the round thunder spots on his chest. The sacred blue stone he tied behind his left ear. He was ready. This was the medicine the *Wakan Tanka* had given him. Now nothing could harm him.

He was not as finely decked out as the others, but he knew that they dressed themselves thus in their finest garb in readiness to meet the Great Spirit looking their best if slain. But he would not be killed he was very sure, so his lack of fine garments did not disturb him.

The warriors remounted their horses and set out at a gallop with Hump at their head. Crazy Horse rode at his side. It was the time for eating meat. Their enemies would all be there. Straight into the heart of the village they charged, scattering people right and left, on across to the other side, circling to charge again.

By this time the startled Gros Ventres had armed and many of them had mounted their horses. Hump with Crazy Horse at his heels circled with shrill "Hi-yi-yis" around the advance guard. Then Hump's horse was shot from under him, throwing him under the noses of the enemy.

The Gros Ventres warriors with upraised war clubs and knives rushed to count coup on the brave Hump. But before they could close in on him, Crazy Horse slid from his horse and boosted his friend onto Strongheart's back, then leaped up behind him. A war club blow intended for his head grazed his shoulder.

Strongheart, who had been trained for this sort of thing, wheeled sharply and was away scattering clods of dirt in the faces of the astounded enemy.

The yipping of the enemy told Crazy Horse that he was being pursued. Strongheart was handicapped with his double load, but he was sturdy and fast and there was a crowd of determined Oglalas galloping to their aid. At length the yells diminished and Crazy Horse allowed his mount to slacken his speed.

"You saved my life," Hump said. "If you had not been there, my scalp would now be hanging from some Gros Ventres' coup stick."

"I am glad I was there," Crazy Horse said simply, but it made a shudder go up his spine at the thought that this great man's scalp could so easily have been taken. "My medicine was good this day," he added.

Hump glanced at the red hawk adorning his head. *"Hau!* Your medicine is good," he agreed. "You must have been granted the vision."

Crazy Horse nodded.

Five Oglala braves rode home carrying enemy scalps that evening. Only one of their number had been injured, and he not seriously.

And that night after the scalp dance when the warriors and others were seated about the campfire, Hump rose to tell of Crazy Horse's brave coup. The other warriors stood up to verify the deed. Everyone looked at Crazy Horse. It was hard to make his face a mask to hide his embarrassment while everyone praised him.

Hump rose again and held up his hand for silence. Then he who was acknowledged the greatest warrior among the Oglalas said solemnly, "This boy, Crazy Horse, who today did this brave deed, will one day be the greatest warrior among all the Lakotas."

Crazy Horse gasped, then sat tense and still for it would be unbecoming for him to show pride or any emotion. But he wondered if he were dreaming, or if he had misheard Hump's statement. However, it was very real. There was the campfire, its flames flickering on the faces all turned in his direction. Across from him sat No Water, his features wearing a sullen expression. This, then, was actually happening to him, Crazy Horse. Never had he imagined anything so amazing — having Hump say that someday he would be the greatest warrior among all of the Lakotas! A great wave of love for Hump swept through him, warming him.

As the meeting broke up and he walked away from the campfire, he was aware of a blanketed figure standing in the shadows. As he approached, folds of the blanket parted and a pair of soft, bright eyes looked straight into his. For the second time that evening Crazy Horse gasped. It was unseemly for an Indian maiden to give a boy her full glance.

Yet, Hopa, the most modest of all Oglala girls, had looked him straight in the eye and in hers he read a depth of admiration. As if overcome by her boldness she shrank back into the shadows.

Crazy Horse went on to his tepee feeling as if he were being borne along upon the wings of an eagle. Never had he felt power so strong in him. Never had he been so sure of himself. It was as if wonderful new adventures were opening before him.

■■■■■■■■■■■

THE
WORST
DEFEAT

T HE EXALTED, set-apart feeling aroused in Crazy Horse by
Hump's statement that he would someday be the greatest
of all Lakota warriors stayed with him the next morning
after he had greeted the rising sun and had partaken of the
first meat of the day. His parents and brother and sister
looked at him with awe as he moved about the tepee. Never
had they known of a boy so young being raised to such a
high position among his people. Already he was great
among the Oglalas. Now soon the word of his greatness
would spread to all of the Teton tribes. It would not have
surprised Crazy Horse to see all of his comrades bow low
as he appeared among them.

He tried not to look self-conscious when he walked out
to meet a group who were getting ready for an arrow shooting contest. He caught up with young Hump, also hurrying to join this group. Hump looked at him with unfriendly eyes, gave a brief greeting, turned and left him.

Crazy Horse was stunned. He stopped momentarily. What had he done to offend his friend? Then it dawned on him what the trouble was. Young Hump was jealous, for it was his own father who had set Crazy Horse into a place of prominence over all other Oglala boys. This realization sobered Crazy Horse. Young Hump's friendship was precious. Would this be one of the prices he had to pay for greatness — the loss of his friends?

He moved more slowly toward the others who were already firing their arrows at a target. Some of them acted rather stiff when he joined them and he did not know quite how to bear himself.

"Here comes the great one," No Water said sarcastically.

"I was proud last night to be your friend," He Dog spoke up quickly.

Crazy Horse looked at him gratefully. All of his friends were not going to abandon him, then. He Dog, at least, was still loyal.

"Line up for your turn," No Water told him curtly. Crazy Horse resented the older boy's tone. He, Crazy Horse, should be the leader giving orders, not No Water. Yet his sense of fair play came to his rescue. He was late in joining the game; it was only right that he should take his turn. He got into line.

And his marksmanship that day was bad. He was one of the poorest in the group, both in hitting the target and in distance shooting. No Water was by far the best of all.

"Our great one, Has-ka, has not the strength of a girl," No Water said scornfully. "I've no doubt that if we had another battle with the wasps he would again cry like a papoose."

Crazy Horse flinched to have the old wound reopened — to hear that detested name again.

"Has-ka is weak today," Brave Bear grinned maliciously.

"Maybe Hump meant that Has-ka's sister would be our great warrior," Lone Hawk put in. "Surely he was wrong about Has-ka's ever being great."

Crazy Horse was hurt by their jibes but knew that it would be a mistake to show resentment. "I will have to improve my marksmanship," he said quietly, "or I will not be able even to keep our stew pot supplied with meat."

He saw the faces of some of his mates soften slightly at these words. They did not want him to put himself above them. He would have to prove himself to them before they accepted his leadership. And the way would not be easy. He realized that now.

On his way back to the tepee he felt a sharp stabbing pain on his left thigh. He stopped and stared down, surprised to see a stream of blood running down his leg. What had happened? He saw an arrow lying in the path before him. He turned, but no one was in sight save some old men dozing in the shade and a group of youngsters splashing in the stream. He limped forward and picked up the arrow and examined it but it told him nothing. The tip was red with his own blood. It bore a hawk feather, but so did dozens of other arrows in camp.

It was only a flesh wound and of no consequence, but it reminded him of his vision in which the red hawk had told him that his worst enemies would be among his own people. *Hau!* This was bad. To have to guard against enemies in his own camp! No, the road to greatness would not be easy. He had scarcely taken the first stumbling step towards its attainment when already someone in his own village sought to harm him. He was very thoughtful as he lifted the flap to his lodge.

He took a small mirror from a bag of knickknacks hang-ing against the rear wall and stared at his reflection, frowning at what he saw. His face was still the soft brown color of an acorn, his hair also was brown and soft instead of the coarse texture and gleaming black an Indian's should be. He had hoped that he would grow darker with age as the buffalo calf did, but now he was at the gateway to manhood and still the "Light-skinned One." No Water had revived the hated name, Has-ka, and he admitted ruefully that it still fitted him.

His father outside the tepee was peeling lengths of wood for arrows. Crazy Horse flopped down on the robe beside him.

"Do I have white blood in my veins?" he asked abruptly.

His father looked up at him, startled. "No," he said. "Why do you ask?"

"My light hair and skin," the boy spat out the words, frowning fiercely as he did so. "Some of the white trappers took Indian wives!"

The holy man shook his head. "You need not bother your head about such a matter," he said with emphasis. "You are a full-blooded Lakota. Your blood is pure."

"Then why am I lighter than the others?"

"It is a distinction of which you can be proud," his father told him. "You know how our people treasure the white buffalo robe — hold the white buffalo sacred."

"Phaugh!" Crazy Horse cried. "What has that to do with me? Who wants in any way to resemble the stinking whites!"

The holy man shrugged. "Young people think it a disgrace to be different from others in the herd," he said in his slow, quiet way. "Yet to stand out, one must be different."

The boy frowned, trying to understand the full meaning of his father's words.

The full days hurried by with the rivalry between Crazy Horse and No Water growing with each passing sun. It was all of the older boy's making, however. Crazy Horse would have been content for matters to take their course without forcing issues, but it was No Water's pleasure to try upon every occasion to make his rival appear at a disadvantage.

One day Crazy Horse was setting out to fish. On his way he ran into No Water with several of his followers. The older boy, with a sneer on his handsome face, planted himself in front of Crazy Horse.

"Our fine friend hoped to avoid his common tribesmen by going off alone again," he cried in a loud voice. "He is so swollen with his own importance that he thinks he is too good to join us in our games."

Crazy Horse stood facing the grinning faces. Always at a loss for words, he felt now as if his tongue were frozen in his mouth.

"You think you are already as great as your friend, the warrior Hump, said you would be." The older boy's tone dripped with scorn. "Your airs make everyone in the tribe double up with laughter. They all know that I, No Water, can best you at any sport."

Anger made Crazy Horse's face hot and words finally came to his tongue.

"You are much given to boasting," he snapped. "Prove what you can do. You choose the sport."

It was a rash challenge. No Water was older, larger and stronger — naturally he was his superior in many things requiring strength.

"*Che-hoo-hoo!*" No Water cried triumphantly. Then without further preliminaries the boys were at each other, struggling, grunting, rolling on the ground, now one on

top, then the other. Crazy Horse fought like a wild cat.
He was quick and agile and No Water was finding him no
easy opponent, but the older boy's strength finally won and
Crazy Horse lay pinned to the ground, helpless and furious
under this new humiliation, for now they were surrounded
by grinning Indians.

No Water enjoyed his triumph and sat bouncing up and
down on his vanquished opponent's chest, laughing and
shouting, "I, No Water, do count coup on the Light-Haired
One, who will never become a warrior because he has the
heart of a girl."

Crazy Horse was to learn, however, that his companions
did not hold his defeat in the wrestling match against him
to any great extent. In fact, a few of them fell away from
No Water in this thing and came over to his side, for they
thought it unfair of the larger boy to challenge one so much
smaller in a sport demanding strength.

The seasons rolled by more or less pleasantly in the fair
land of the Big Horns. The Crows, whose land this had
been, were still resentful of having the Sioux take over their
fine country and there were numerous battles. Crazy Horse
now was an accepted warrior and had added greatly to his
collection of coups. Time and again he was pushed forward
about the campfire to tell of his exploits. But he sat down
quickly and did not speak. Others, however, spoke for him.
But there was nothing shy about No Water. Now he had
also gained coups and he was strong of voice in telling about
them. He had three scalps dangling from his stick to dance
around during the victory dance. But Crazy Horse scorned
the taking of scalps unless it was necessary to kill the enemy
to save his own or a comrade's life.

"I prefer to strike the living enemy," he said quietly one

day to his brother, Little Hawk, who chided him for not having a collection of scalps at least equal to No Water's.

Four snows had passed since the time the Oglalas had moved away from the white man's fort on the Platte. Crazy Horse's hatred of the Blue Coats had faded as his memory of them dimmed. It was all like some long-forgotten nightmare. Now and then news walkers came to tell of the doings of the white men. No longer did the fast riding boys gallop over the plains with their bags filled with folded papers. Instead there was a new and magic way of sending words — stranger even than the black marks on white

paper. The white men planted rows of trees without branches across the plains and strung singing wires between them. Those wires carried their words from pole to pole, clear from the White Father in Washington. The news walker said that he had stood with his ear against one of the branchless trees of the singing wires, but could hear nothing.

Crazy Horse thought that he would like to see such a thing. Truly some of the white men's ways were powerful. But he was in no hurry to move away from this fine country where life was interesting and exciting, with battles against the Crows, horse stealing, hunting — all of the things that made Indian life good. He had gained many ponies himself, most of which he gave away, for he had no wish for wealth. At present he had a gun taken from a Crow warrior and a fine lance, also taken from the enemy.

The news walker had said most of the soldiers at the fort had gone back to the land of their Father, for the whites were fighting among themselves.

"Now," said some of the young warriors, "will be a good time to make war upon the fort with so few there to hold it."

But the idea did not appeal to many. Life was too good here in the north.

Crazy Horse was aware of a change which had taken place in many of his comrades. Now some of them were interested in standing under the blanket in the Indian manner of courtship with the Oglala maidens. He still felt warm around the heart whenever he knew that Hopa's shy eyes were upon him, but he was not ready for courtship and marriage yet. First he must become a great warrior, then he would tie his finest horses before the lodge of Hopa's father. There was still time for that sort of thing. Anyway, he was busy now training his brother, Little Hawk, in the ways of warfare.

Red Cloud was leading a band of his finest warriors against the Crows and Little Hawk had begged to go along. This would be his first big battle.

The two boys set out with the warrior band while the women sang songs as they rode through the village. Each rode a fast horse and led another. Crazy Horse carried his gun. Little Hawk had a strong new bow his older brother had made for him and a quiver full of new arrows.

It was a strong, good fight and Little Hawk, like his older brother, won his coups by choosing the braver method of striking the living enemy rather than taking scalps to boast about.

But when they returned to camp, Crazy Horse did not take part in the victory dance held that night; nor did he even listen to the good talk about the coups his younger brother had made. He crept off into the hills alone, like a wounded animal. For he had come home to news that made him sick in the middle. While he was away fighting the Crows, No Water had put his blanket around Hopa and led her off to the lodge of his father. Now she was his wife.

At first Crazy Horse could not believe this thing. He had always planned that someday Hopa would sit in his own tepee making his moccasins. Had he been wrong in reading in her shy glances knowledge of his plans? Now she belonged to another. To his rival. This was worse than any hurt — any pain or sickness he had ever known. And there was nothing that the medicine man — or anyone else could do about it.

BAD

TIDINGS

13

CRAZY HORSE went to the hills where he stayed alone with his dark thoughts. When he returned once more to eat meat with his family, his father clumsily tried to comfort him. "It was her father gave her away to No Water," he said.

Crazy Horse was silent, frowning.

"Because of the many horses he tied before his tepee," the holy man went on. "And because No Water makes such loud noise about his coups in the meetings. You sit silent, yet you have more honors than any young warrior among the Oglalas. You have taken more horses, yet you give them all away."

"A truly big man does not talk of his own coups," the young man said. "And one whose heart is good gives away his wealth to the needy; he does not keep it for himself or for show-off purposes."

The old man nodded his head in agreement but his eyes were sad for the hurt that he knew was in his son's heart.

Life had been good in the Powder River country during four snows, but now suddenly everything was bitter for Crazy Horse. He threw himself into every battle against the Crows, the Snakes and the Gros Ventres, always out in the lead, as if daring death to touch him, but the enemy bullets and arrows had no power against him.

"Never have the Oglalas seen such a warrior!" the men said around the campfires, but Crazy Horse was not there to hear himself praised. He had become a lone wolf among the Lakotas, and more than ever the "Silent One."

Now that one bad thing had happened, others followed in its wake. First came messengers bearing orders from the white agent for the Oglalas to come to the fort for a pow-wow. Crazy Horse, remembering the bad things which had happened to his people at the hands of the whites, made himself stand up in council to speak against going. But his uncle, Spotted Tail, who had been held prisoner in the soldiers' fort for two snows rose and said that the Oglalas must go. The might of the white men was too strong for the Indians to resist.

Some leaders spoke for continuing the good Indian life here in the hills where there were no white men, but others remembered what had happened to the camp of Little Thunder when he had refused to move when the soldier chief told him to do so, and finally the tepees were taken down and the slow procession trailed south toward the fort. Reaching the Holy Road they found bunches of soldiers in all of the little stations where the fast riding boys used to change horses. It looked bad.

Marching along beside the road were the bare poles along which were strung the mysterious "talking wires" about

which the news walkers had told. Crazy Horse stood with
his ear against one of the dead trees, trying to hear spoken
words. Then some of the young men threw their lariats
over one of the poles and with their horses pulled it to the
ground. They cut the wires and put them to their ears, but
still could hear nothing.

While they camped near Fort Laramie they would have
to eat the white men's "whoa haws" (cattle) which they detested, for there were no buffalo for many miles.

One of the news walkers came into camp with talk of why
this was so. Even far off the trail where the herds had been
driven, the white hunters were destroying them by the
thousands, taking only the hides to pile high in their big
wagons, leaving the entire carcasses to rot on the prairie.
The Oglalas set up a moaning at such wanton destruction.

While the Indians waited at the fort for the white agent
to come up the Holy Road with his wagons of presents from
the Great White Father, other bad things were told by the
news walkers who were now kept busy traveling from camp
to camp with the ever-increasing evil tidings. The one
called Bozeman rode out from the north country to the fort
with a wagonload of stakes. Ever so often he would stop
his horses and get down from the wagon and drive a stake
in the ground. Crazy Horse was with the handful of warriors who rode out to watch from the hilltop as he did this
strange thing. Right through the heart of their hunting
ground he went.

"Let them go," Crazy Horse said when one of the rash
young men would have gone forth to take Bozeman's scalp.
"He is leaving our country. Do not stir up trouble because of one harmless man."

Loafer Indians who had remained around the fort sent
word that the Bozeman wagon train was going north to the

land of the Crows for the bright dirt which drove white men crazy. Soon many others would follow, as always happened when the word "gold" was spoken.

Alarm ran through the village. The Lakotas had left the Holy Road in peace, according to their agreement, and in spite of the bad things which had happened to their people whenever they came in contact with the white men. Now the gold seekers were pushing a road through their last hunting ground. The Oglalas knew what would happen. The game would be driven away; the hunting spoiled; the white men would take possession of their lands. This must not happen!

The warriors readied their weapons, took bags of *wasna* and set out to follow the Bozeman wagon train and every night signal fires blazed from the hilltops, summoning the Miniconjous, the Hunkpapas and even the northern Cheyennes whose troubles with the whites had been many.

Three sleeps from the fort the Bozeman wagons found themselves completely surrounded by scowling warriors sitting silently astride their ponies, out of gunshot, with rifles and bows and arrows ready. A smile quirked at the corners of Crazy Horse's lips to see the women scampering around the white man's camp like frightened sage hens, the men gathering in knots, motioning with their arms.

It was agreed that no hostile action would be taken unless the white men started it; the Sioux would simply bar the way to their hunting grounds. Several sleeps passed without the train's trying to break through the "surround." Then two white men were seen by the night outposts trying to sneak through to the soldier fort.

"Let them go," Crazy Horse said. "We will watch what they do."

Often now his warriors looked to him to tell them what

action to take. His words were quiet and few, but it made his heart pound to realize that they bore weight with the people. These things which had happened since they moved back to the Holy Road had taken his mind from the aching sickness left when Hopa had gone to the lodge of No Water. He seldom thought of her now; warrior affairs were of more importance.

Signals flashed that the two white men had reached the Holy Road and had used the talking wires to the fort. Soon horse soldiers — many of them — set out from the fort, riding fast toward the Bozeman train. Indian signal fires burned at night summoning still more warriors. Then it was seen that the soldiers were leading all of the whites back to the fort.

"Let them go," said Crazy Horse. "So long as they turn back we will not make trouble. But we will be ready if they try again."

"*Hau!*" agreed his warriors. This was good advice.

No more wagon trains came over the staked trail and the Oglalas moved camp near Bear Butte in the Black Hills country. Then the snows came, shutting them in their snug village. No more was heard about the whites until the next summer when news walkers came to tell of another bad thing which had happened on the Holy Road. A party of Miniconjous and Hunkpapas crossing the road came upon an emigrant train. They stopped to smoke and to eat meat with the people. They were ready to ride away when a messenger came bringing news that the soldier chief on the river called the Missouri had killed some of their people and put their heads up on poles.

This was too much for the Sioux to bear. In reprisal they shot some of the emigrants, burned the wagons and took two women and a little girl as captives, then hurried north to join their people.

"That is not good!" Crazy Horse cried angrily. "The Miniconjous and Hunkpapas acted foolishly. That is not the way to fight the whites. These things must be planned. Now we must stand together."

Some of his followers frowned at these words. A warrior must avenge the death of his people. It was the Sioux way. Such things could not be planned, for many words made actions weak. Was he, too, turning away from the Indian way of fighting?

"Has-ka should stay with the women while men go out to do the fighting," No Water said with a scornful smile.

Rage filled the heart of Crazy Horse. Ever since he had taken Hopa to his lodge, No Water had avoided his old-time rival. Now he was again growing bold with his taunts. But Crazy Horse held down his anger and ignored No Water. This was no time for personal rivalries; there were bigger matters to deal with.

Then came word so bad that it caused all else to be forgotten like a flood sweeping everything from its path. The Cheyenne chiefs, Black Kettle and White Antelope, had settled their peaceful village on Sand Creek, the place where their agent told them to camp. Then the soldier chief called Chivington, an Indian hater with a heart hot for killings, brought his command swooping upon the peaceful, sleeping village and blasted it to bits, killing men, women and children as they tried to flee to the hills.

Crazy Horse stood in the midst of his people as they listened speechless to the words the news walker spilled from his mouth.

"Ey-ee-ee!" the keening sound broke from the throats of the women. These were not their own people who had died. But now it was as if all Indians were one nation. What had happened to one band could easily happen to all. What would become of them?

Such rage and hatred welled up in Crazy Horse that he could not speak. He strode away from the crowd to a lone hilltop. A hawk was circling in the blue sky. He watched it until the lazy, graceful motions eased the tumult in his heart.

Finally he stretched out his arms and sent his spirit to the *Wakan Tanka.* He stood thus in yearning silence — and then it happened. The vision came again in a din of crashing thunder and dazzling lightning. He was astride a black stallion painted with thunder dots and zigzag lightning streaks. He was leading his people who were fighting as a unit under his direction. And all about Blue Coats lay on the ground, dead.

The Vision faded away slowly, but the feeling of strength it left in him remained. And the echoes of the words spoken echoed and re-echoed in his brain. "You are powerful among the Sioux," the Voice had said. "But the power is not given you for personal gain. It is for the good of the people."

Crazy Horse walked with long strides back to the village.

"We must all unite," he told his people in ringing tones. "Not only our own tribes of Sioux, but other Plains nations must join with us. We must fight as do the Blue Coats. We will drive them from our land."

So firm was his voice and so confident his bearing that his people looked at him with respect and a chorus of *"haus"* came from the warriors and even the old men.

Later, when the Cheyennes came bearing the war pipe, he was the first in his band to smoke.

"Come with us," he told the Cheyennes bearing the pipe. "When all of our people met here by Bear Butte in the summer of White Bear Holding, our numbers were like the buffalo herds of the time of our fathers. We are strong. Let the soldiers come!"

A new wave of excitement ran through the camp at his words. If the soldiers came for trouble, the Sioux would let them have it. They would drive the white people from the plains. The land of the Indians would be their own again. And when the white men were gone the buffalo herds would return once more.

Ho-hechetu! Life would be good then!

THEY
SHALL
NOT
COME
HERE!

■■■■■■■ 14

CRAZY HORSE knew that the Cheyennes had in their camp two white women whom they had taken from a wagon train after the Chivington Massacre. Although he knew that this was a bad thing to do, he did not blame the Cheyennes who had suffered so much from the Blue Coats.

The Chivington affair united the Oglalas on the question of what had to be done. All agreed that there must be a fight to the finish. Even Spotted Tail, who ever since his return from the soldiers' jail had held out against opposing the whites, now said that his people must make a stand.

Words did not come easily to the tongue of Crazy Horse, now twenty snows old, but with his mind so hot with hatred, his words in council were loud and strong. He did not talk on and on for the pleasure of hearing his voice as some did; his words were few and to the point. The whites must be driven from the plains. The Sioux must learn to fight in a body as the soldiers did, and for the good of the people instead of for individual honors.

As he spoke he felt as if he were pouring something from himself into his people. It was a good feeling.

When he sat down he noticed that even the old men nodded in agreement with what he said. His few plain statements bore more weight than did the oratory of some of the more talkative ones.

Finally it was decided in council that the Sioux would fight as Crazy Horse advised — in a body instead of the old way of striving for coups.

It was the Middle of the Winter Moon when the Arapahoes who had also smoked the war pipe offered by the Cheyennes met with the Lakotas and Cheyennes on Beaver Creek. Crazy Horse, riding up on his spotted pony, felt his heart grow big with pride as he saw the lodges of all those who had come to council stretch far back into the hills.

When the war party, one thousand strong, set out to strike the first blow in vengeance for the murder of the Cheyennes on Sand Creek, Crazy Horse wanted to shout with wild joy. He had never before seen such a company of Indians riding together and it reminded him of the old-time buffalo herd in number.

Ho-hechetu! It was well! The Plains Indians were strong. The white men could never drive them from the land of their fathers.

Crazy Horse pulled off to one side to watch the fine procession file by and his eyes shone with excitement at the sight. The war chiefs or pipe bearers in their best war finery rode out in front. The warriors, among whom Crazy Horse had been riding, came next. The *akicita* guarded the flanks and rear, to prevent the reckless young men from galloping out.

It was good to see such a strong body set out in a column as for an old-time tribal hunt. Because the Lakotas had been the first to smoke the pipe, they were given the honor of riding at the head. It was early in the Moon of Snow-blindness when they reached the region near Julesburg, a stage station and soldier post. They hid in the hills to the south. That night there was a war dance.

When the dance was over an old man walked about the circle shouting, "Co-oo-ee! Seven of our bravest young warriors of all the tribes will be chosen. They are to act as decoys in the morning, to lead the Blue Coats into ambush!"

Crazy Horse's heart skipped a beat. This was his own plan which he had explained in the council. The old men had actually adopted it. He stood at one side, in the background, curious to see who had been picked to act as the decoys, and who the leader of this brave band would be.

Glancing across the crowd he saw No Water standing out well in front so that he would be noticed. He appeared to be very confident that he was one the old men had chosen.

The crier shouted six names, but No Water's was not among them. The old man stopped in the center of the circle and shouted, "The leader of this courageous band is our brave young warrior who is wise beyond his years. Who thinks more of the welfare of his people than he does for personal honors: Crazy Horse!"

Following this announcement the people shouted for joy.

Crazy Horse gasped at hearing his own name spoken for this honor, but he made his face a mask so that his pride would not show through.

In the morning he readied himself for battle by tying on his red hawk headdress, hanging the sacred stone behind his ear, twisting his hair in a knot on one side of his head,

and painting his face with the lightning zigzag and his chest with round dots. He also painted the lightning and thunder marks upon the rump of his fast Crow pony.

He rode out at the head of his picked band, singing his war song:

> *Comrades, kinsmen,*
> *Now have ye spoken thus,*
> *The earth is mine,*
> *'Tis my domain.*
> *'Tis said, and now I exert me!*

The six young warriors followed close behind. When they came to the edge of Julesburg they galloped back and forth yelling and whooping. Soon cavalrymen from Fort Rankin came galloping toward them. Crazy Horse led his band in the direction of the hills, hoping the soldiers would think they were scared off and would follow. His plan was to let the Blue Coats almost catch them and to lead them over the hill where the rest of the Indians were waiting. But before the trap could be sprung, some of the younger warriors slipped past the *akicita* and rushed pell-mell to count coup on the soldiers. The cavalrymen whirled and raced back toward the fort with the entire Indian force close upon their heels. The old men and women and older boys followed, bringing extra ponies.

The troopers and all of those at the station ran for safety inside the heavy-walled stockade. Fourteen of the frightened Blue Coats did not gain the safety of the stockade. Indian arrows brought them down. Then with much triumphant yelling the Indians ransacked the store, loaded the extra horses with hams, bacons, sacks of flour, and sugar and bolts of cloth until all that could be seen of the animals was their legs and noses. Crazy Horse joined in the fun and found a strong box which he had to break open with strong tools. He was disappointed to find inside only bundles of the queer green paper like that which he had seen when Spotted Tail's young men attacked the box wagon.

The warriors set out late in the day for their own camps. The younger ones grabbed the ends of the bolts of cloth, as they urged their ponies into a gallop. The cloth unraveled, making bright streaks of color across the prairie as the billowing streamers floated out. When the bolts were unraveled the braves roped the talking poles with the cloth and pulled the wires to the ground.

That night there was a scalp dance, but Crazy Horse took no part.

It was a sorry affair, with only fourteen scalps to dance around. He was sick with disgust that his carefully planned surround had been spoiled by the reckless young men greedy for personal honors. Only fourteen scalps taken when every white man who showed his face outside the fort should have been killed! Would their rash young warriors ever learn to fight for the good of the people?

The white men, though, need not think that the Julesburg raid was the end of trouble for them. The Indian warriors went into council and it was decided to move north to the Powder River, and to cut a wide path of destruction along the Platte as they went.

"Spare no one," Crazy Horse ordered, as his people got ready for the March of Death. "Remember the news our friends, the Cheyennes, brought, that the white chief Chivington ordered his men to kill women and children as well as warriors, for 'lice make nits.' We shall see to it that no white lice are left to breed their kind."

They rode forth. They swooped upon every ranch, upon

every station, every wagon train. The young men's lust for
killing grew as they traveled along the Holy Road, burning buildings and wagons, cutting telegraph poles, firing
the stage stations where frightened white people had taken
refuge. It was as if a giant fire swept across the plains,
leaving a wide path of black death.

At night war drums throbbed. Long lines of campfires
blazed on the hilltops. But the soldiers stayed cooped up
within their stockades and did nothing. The Indian camps
were overcrowded with captured cattle and the victorious
redskins grew fat from feasting on foodstuff they had taken.
Best of all, they had gained many guns and much ammunition.

Before they left the Platte to move north to the hunting
grounds, the warriors once again swooped upon Julesburg.
Again Crazy Horse and his six picked men rode out planning to entice the soldiers into an ambush. But the troops
had learned their lesson and would not rise to the same
bait a second time.

"*Hukahey!*" Crazy Horse shouted. "They are cowards.
Let them shiver inside their walls. We will build a fire to
warm them!"

Lighting a firebrand, he led his band in burning the
houses and trading post of the little settlement. As he saw
the red flames leap up from the buildings and haystacks,
some of their heat entered the veins of Crazy Horse. Never
would his hatred for the white men die down as those flames
he was watching soon would die. Never, he vowed, would
he cease fighting them until the last one lay dead.

After that last skirmish the triumphant Indians moved
their great village across the Platte River now turned to
ice, to begin their trek north. There were nearly a thousand lodges, by the white man's count, with many women

and children and a large herd of captured animals. The trail they made across the snowy country was plain to see, for any troops who cared to follow, but none did.

It was a slow journey, with so many to move, but at last they came to the Powder River country where some of the northern Oglalas had stayed, unaware that their southern relatives had smoked the pipe with the Cheyennes and the Arapahoes. They were greatly impressed by the amount of loot brought in and they, with great enthusiasm, joined in the feasting and the victory scalp dances.

Yet there was disunity in camp. Some of those who had remained in the Powder River country still talked for peace with the whites. One of their chiefs, Man-Afraid, was among these.

"Stay away from the white men," he fiercely told his warriors. "Do not go looking for trouble. Stay far away from their road."

Crazy Horse was disappointed in Man-Afraid, who once had been one of his heroes, and whose quiet way he had tried to imitate. Man-Afraid had not seen the many bad things the white soldiers did, or he would not talk so strong for peace. Yet, as the days slipped back into their pleasant routine of hunting, with now and then a raid on the Crows, the flaming heat in Crazy Horse's veins cooled and he thought less and less about the white men. There was much feasting, much visiting between the camps, much social dancing.

After Hopa had moved into the lodge of No Water, Crazy Horse had thought that he would never look at another woman. But now there was a Cheyenne girl who often tossed the pebble at his feet during the social dances. Pleased, he picked it up and became her partner. Often she came to walk beneath the robe with him. Perhaps he should think of going out on a pony stealing raid so that he would have horses to tie in front of her father's lodge.

The Oglalas looked coldly upon him for going so often to visit the Cheyenne camp. Were not the Oglala girls good enough for him, they asked. But his eyes took on a cold look when he was opposed which seemed to raise a frigid barrier that made his opponents shrink into themselves. And he continued his visits to the other village.

Then something happened to make him forget again the soft look in a woman's eyes. A news walker brought in the word which again set the entire camp in an uproar.

Crazy Horse knew that when one of the wagon trains had been attacked after the Julesburg raid, the Cheyennes had carried off a white woman captive who called herself Mrs. Eubank. The Oglalas did not care for this Cheyenne habit of taking white women — silly, weak creatures who cried most of the time and who could not tan hides or carry much wood or even set up a tepee. Two Face, an Oglala chief, who had always been friendly to the whites, bought the white woman from the Cheyennes, for five horses, and he set out to return her to the soldiers at Laramie. On the way he met another friendly chief, Blackfoot, whom he persuaded to accompany him.

Upon reaching the fort the two chiefs turned the white woman over to the soldier chief. Instead of giving them presents for the good thing they had done, the white chief had his soldiers put chains about the necks of the two friendly chiefs and had them lifted up to hang until dead. Their bodies dangled outside the fort for all to see, while the soldiers with spear guns walked back and forth so that their own people could not come and cut them down.

When Crazy Horse heard of this new bad thing the whites had done, the hate which had died down to smouldering embers flamed up again stronger than ever. It was as if each new evil the soldiers did was like a blast of wind blowing his hatred to a hotter pitch. What would come of it all?

"Follow me!" No Water shouted, riding through the camp. "All who are brave ride with me to make war upon the whites. We will take their scalps — "

Many of the reckless young warriors were eager to follow No Water.

"Wait!" Crazy Horse galloped up to stop the wild braves. "You cannot do this. A handful of warriors so poorly armed as you, no matter how brave, would only throw away your lives before the Blue Coats' guns."

"Wait! Wait!" No Water spat out the words scornfully. "Brave men do not fear to die. Crazy Horse is a coward."

"Everyone knows Crazy Horse is no coward." He Dog's voice rose above the hubbub of sound.

"Only a fool throws his life away," Crazy Horse spoke calmly but with a ring of authority to his voice. "We must wait. We must learn to fight together for the good of our people. We must get more white men's guns."

Finally, he persuaded the reckless ones to bide their time.

But now was not the time to think about soldier troubles. It was time for the Sun Dance ceremonials, then time for the fall hunts to make fat the *parfleches* (hide bags), and to make much meat for hanging from high branches for winter eating.

Before the spring grass had put fat back on the ponies' ribs, a runner came from Laramie bringing news that soldiers' camps were thicker than spring flowers around the fort. There was talk, too, that the soldiers — more even than were in the old-time buffalo herds — would soon move north to drive the Sioux away from the Powder River country. Even here, far away from the Holy Road, were not the Lakotas to be safe from molestation by the whites? Even here the soldiers must come killing, dragging their wagon guns!

"They shall not come!" Crazy Horse's voice was hoarse like the growl of a wounded grizzly. "This is our country. Our hunting ground! Here we will make our stand. Here we will fight for what is our own. Fight until not a white man is left. The time has come!"

POWDER
RIVER
EXPEDITION
■■■■■■■ 15

THE RUSTLE OF ALARM which ran through the camps after the news walker's message was like the wind stirring dry leaves. There were those among the old men who thought it would be best to move again — to a safer place.

"Where is such a place?" Crazy Horse demanded angrily, as he stalked through the village talking to the people. "No matter where we go the whites come. It is not enough that we camp far, far from their Holy Road. It is not enough that we have nothing to do with them. We are many now," he waved his arm, taking in the vast stretch of tepees, for the seven tribes of the Lakotas still remained in one big camp, and many of the Cheyennes stayed near by.

In the council Crazy Horse spoke loud for united action in fighting.

"The time of fighting for personal honors is gone forever," he shouted. "The good of our people is what we

159

must think of now. We must fight in a body — as the Blue
Coats do — under a single leader — "

Red Cloud, the war chief, nodded. *"Hau!* Our warrior,
Crazy Horse, is right," he agreed. "We must fight under
one leader."

Yet when word came that the soldiers were near, the
Indians would not carry out such a plan and broke into
little bands.

Vainly Crazy Horse galloped from group to group.

"Our force is weak," he argued. "We have only as many
guns as the fingers on one hand, and our bows and arrows
against the soldiers' better weapons. We must lead them
into ambush. Stampede their horses. When we have them
afoot, we can slay them."

The warriors pretended to agree, but then dashed out in
groups down the Powder River to meet the soldiers, without waiting for the decoys to act.

When these rash ones talked of their deeds around the
campfire that night, a chilly silence told them that the old
way of counting coup was no longer in favor. The people
wanted Crazy Horse's way of fighting.

There were other skirmishes with the Blue Coats, which
did not amount to much except to furnish sport for the
Sioux and to allow Crazy Horse to drill them in their new
tactics, and from these fights they gained hundreds of horses
and mules and some new guns.

When the first light snow fell in the mountains, the
Indians' time and attention was taken up by hunting for
winter meat. The meat made, the tribes moved together
for the big matter which was now being talked of in every
tepee — the organization of a new Chief's society, one which
would be powerful over all the others. Its members would
be leaders of all the people. Once there had been such a

society, but it had fallen apart — disintegrated as so many things had when the Lakotas came in contact with the whites. Now that troubled times had come, the people needed strong leaders as they had never needed them before. For this reason the head men of the Oglalas decided to revive the once strong society of Shirt Wearers.

When the subject had been discussed around the council fires the people had agreed to accept the leadership of such a society. There would be seven old men leaders, called Big Bellies, and four young warriors, or Shirt Wearers, the true leaders of the people in all things. For days all that the Indians could talk about was, who would the four young warriors be?

"The Big Bellies will choose their own sons," the father of Crazy Horse said. "It is natural enough. It has always been so. If I were one of the head chiefs, I would no doubt choose my older son."

"It is well you are not a chief," Crazy Horse said quietly. "I would not want to be chosen because my father was a Big Belly. A man should advance on his own merits."

The holy man nodded. He had sensed Crazy Horse's boyhood resentment that his father was not a chief, or at least a warrior. Crazy Horse had truly shed his young traits — had taken on manly characteristics which made the holy man proud of him.

"Many of the young warriors look to you for leadership," he told his son. "Your medicine is good. There is still time to earn greater honors."

"*Hau!*" Crazy Horse agreed absently.

He saw women busy clearing away the sage and brush on a level stretch of land. A big circle was being made. Then the large council lodge was erected. His father as holy man had helped paint on this ceremonial lodge the sun and moon and buffalo and other sacred symbols of the people.

The big day dawned warm and sunny, the air was clear and stimulating. Birds were singing, even wild animals came to the edge of the camp to stare curiously, as though they knew that this was an important, sacred day and that they would be safe.

The sides of the big lodge were rolled up so that all could see what took place inside. The heralds of the Big Bellies dressed in their finest war garb rode out on painted ponies to point out which of the four young men were to be honored above all others of the Lakota nation.

One of the riders stopped beside Young-Man-Afraid-of-His-Horses. A great "ahhh!" of admiration rose from the crowd and everyone repeated his name. Then Sword, son of Chief Brave Bear was chosen; then American Horse, son of Sitting Bear.

The father of Crazy Horse made a shield of his hand and said behind it, "It is as I said. The Big Bellies choose their own sons to honor."

Crazy Horse was standing with his family on the edge of the crowd. "They are brave men," he said quietly. "It should not be held against them that their fathers are chiefs."

He was looking at his father as he spoke and was surprised by the expression on the old man's face — one of mingled amazement, disbelief and joy. He turned to see what his father was looking at. There was one of the Big Bellies' heralds at his shoulder.

"Crazy Horse," said the rider, "you are one chosen to be a Shirt Wearer — a leader of the people."

His heart almost stopped beating. He felt himself being lifted to the horse behind the herald. He heard such a roar from the crowd that he was nearly deafened. His own name was repeated over and over.

"Ahhh!" he heard. "Crazy Horse is chosen because he is great — not because his father is a Big Belly."

He was taken to the council lodge and told to seat himself on the white buffalo robe in the center. The old men chiefs sat in the outer circle. There was feasting on buffalo meat and venison and the old men leaders stood up to tell why each of the four young men had been chosen. Crazy Horse's ears burned with the praise he heard of himself. Feeling the eyes of all of the people upon him, he wished that he could bury himself beneath the robe upon which he sat, but he kept his eyes staring straight ahead and acted as though he could not hear what was being said.

Then the pipe was passed and solemnly smoked by the seven old men chiefs and by the chosen four who were then asked to rise. The old men brought forth four beautifully embroidered skin bags. From these they drew the shirts they had made with their own hands, of bighorn sheepskins. Each shirt had quill embroidery and painted on the skins were pictures of the brave deeds done by the young man who was to wear it.

After the shirts were donned a single eagle feather was stuck in the back of the headband of each Shirt Wearer. Then there was more feasting after which the drums commenced to throb as a signal for the dancing.

Crazy Horse kept his eyes lowered as his moccasins shuffled on the hard ground. He was aware that many pebbles were dropping at his feet — invitations from the maidens for him to be their partner, but he pretended not to notice them. He had never taken part in social or courtship dancing. He had no heart for it now, but since he had

been shoved forward into such prominence he felt that he would appear ungrateful of the honor if he shrank into the background.

At length, however, he became aware of a pair of eyes staring at him, willing him to raise his own. Curiously, he did so, to gaze straight into the dark eyes of Hopa, the woman he had once planned to have as his wife, but whom No Water had carried off. There was a pleading look in her eyes — as if she were striving to say something — or to be understood.

Crazy Horse was amazed. This was not the way of a modest Indian woman — for the wife of one man to give her eyes thus boldly to another. Yet for a moment he had a wild impulse to leap to her side. To seize her and to fold her blanket closely about both of them to shield them from the view of others. But he dropped his eyes and continued to shuffle the steps of the dance alone.

CIRCLE

OF

DEATH

■■■■■■■■ 16

Sadness hung over the Teton camp, for the daughter of Spotted Tail was dying of the white man's coughing sickness. It had been a bitter winter of deep snows and piercing cold. The Indians had lost many ponies and had run short of food, so when a messenger came saying that the white chief at the fort had a new peace paper for the chiefs to sign and would give many presents including guns, some of the people were in favor of going.

"More peace papers!" Crazy Horse raged. "What have their peace papers ever meant? It is better to starve, if we must, here in our own land rather than go in to be put behind bars in the white man's jails, or to be hung up by the neck as if we were buffalo carcasses."

Most of his people agreed with him. Spotted Tail, though, insisted upon taking his daughter to the fort so that she could be buried near her grandfather, Old Smoke.

The messengers, too, had brought word that the Brulés had already signed a paper giving away the land for a road through the Powder River country, along the trail where Bozeman had set stakes. The yellow metal which drove white men crazy had been found north of the Powder River country. That was why the white men wanted the new road.

"More of the white man's lies," Crazy Horse scoffed when he heard that the Brulés had signed away their land.

The Brulés had not come north with the other tribes but surely they would not be guilty of signing away the land of their cousins — not even for the white man's presents. There were those, though, who believed the report and when Spotted Tail set out to carry his dying daughter to the fort, many followed him. Red Cloud was among those eager to go.

"Are you so eager for the white man's presents?" Crazy Horse asked scornfully. "Have you forgotten the bad things that always come to our people from the whites?"

Red Cloud's eyes refused to meet those of the younger man. "It is necessary that we must find out the truth about the road."

There was a chorus of "*haus*" of agreement to Red Cloud's statement. Crazy Horse wanted to stay in the Powder River country where life was good, but, seeing that so many of his people were determined to go with Spotted Tail to the fort, he got on his horse and rode with them.

Red Cloud's tongue was always full of good-sounding words, so the Shirt Wearers pushed him forward to be their spokesman when they met with the white soldiers inside a tent near the fort.

The white man chief called Many Deer brought out the white peace paper to show to Red Cloud, Man-Afraid and

Crazy Horse. He pointed to the scrawls which he said were
the names of the Brulé chief, Swift Bear, and others, mainly
Loafers Around the Fort. But when he showed them marks
which he said made the name of their own Spotted Tail, the
Oglala leaders looked at each other in amazement.

"He put his hand to the pen as soon as he came to the
fort with his daughter," Many Deer told them.

"Spotted Tail did not know what he was doing," Red
Cloud said. "Spotted Tail is a good man." He then insisted that the white chief explain every detail of the agreement.

"This treaty applies to an old road," the white chief said.

"Not to the trail of the stakes?" Red Cloud asked.

"No. To an old road," the white man repeated, but his
eyes did not meet those of the Indian.

Crazy Horse pointed to a great cloud of dust rising over
the Holy Road.

"What is that?" he demanded.

Many Deer, pretending not to hear, went on talking of
other things.

Crazy Horse jerked his head in a signal for the Shirt
Wearers and some of his other followers to go with him.
They went to the top of a knoll and saw a large body of
troops marching up the North Platte.

A frown creased the brow of Crazy Horse. More soldiers
marching up the Holy Road even while the peace talk was
going on! What could it mean?

He turned to one of his Brulé friends who had followed
him. "You are known to be friendly to the whites," he
said. "When those Blue Coats make camp, go among them
and find out why they are here."

Crazy Horse and his friends returned to the peace talk
being held in a large lodge with a small speaker's platform

in the center. While the meeting was still going on, Colonel Carrington, chief of the Blue Coats who had just come up the Holy Road, strode into the lodge.

Crazy Horse felt a prickle of excitement run up his spine at sight of the soldier chief, but he kept his eyes straight ahead.

A few moments later the Brulé he had sent out to spy lifted the flap of the lodge and whispered in Crazy Horse's ear, "I learned in the soldier camp that the Blue Coats are on their way to the Powder River country. They are sent there by the White Father in Washington to build a fort to protect the Bozeman Trail for those on their way to dig the shining earth."

Red Cloud, seated beside Crazy Horse, had heard the whispered words of the spy. With a roar of rage Red Cloud leaped to his feet and jumped onto the platform. Pointing to the silver eagle on Colonel Carrington's shoulder straps, he shouted, "There is the White Eagle sent to steal a road through our land. Do not sign the lying white paper, my people!" Springing from the platform, he shouted, "Take down the tepees. Follow me!"

There were those who lingered behind to get the presents offered by the white chief, but the young braves followed Red Cloud and Crazy Horse who set out on a gallop for the Powder River country.

The Shirt Wearers went around to all of the tribes which had scattered for hunting, carrying the war pipe to them and telling them of the many Blue Coats who were coming to their land. The Cheyennes had gone back to the Black Hills and runners were sent to tell them the news. While the travois were moving toward the encampment on the Little Goose River, the soldiers under Carrington marched straight across the country to Little Piney Creek, a branch

of the Powder River. Soon the rasping noise of saws, the
sound of axes and the pounding hammers of men at work
building a fort made discord in the once quiet country.

"This is our last hunting ground," Crazy Horse cried.
"They are building a fort in the very heart of it. There is
nowhere else for us to go. We must drive them away!"

The thought was with him constantly. He knew the
climax was not far off. They must drive the Blue Coats
from their land or perish.

Over and over he repeated his words and with such force
that everyone listened and many agreed that now they must
make a last stand of desperation. Crazy Horse knew that
they would be fighting soldiers well equipped with carbines
and wagon guns.

"You must listen to me," Crazy Horse told his warriors.
"We must change our way of fighting. We must have a plan
of action. We must drill. Learn to fight as a unit instead
of for individual honors."

At first the young warriors grumbled at his words.

"You will do as your leaders say. You will follow my plan
or look for a new leader," Crazy Horse said it calmly but
there was a force behind his words which made the young
warriors regard him with respect. They saw a firm look
which gave them confidence in him. This was the test of
his leadership. If he could not get the young men to change
their manner of fighting, he was not their leader. He must
not fail, for if he did, his people were lost.

Back in the hills he had his warriors drill, following
blanket signals from the leaders on a hilltop.

"It is like a boy's game." Some of the warriors sulked
and refused to drill.

"It is a game which succeeds well for the Blue Coats,"
Crazy Horse retorted.

He sent these sulky warriors to make small raids upon the gold seekers who came up the new road called the Bozeman Trail. Crazy Horse knew this was a wise thing to do. It kept the soldiers reminded of the Sioux's vow not to allow the white men through their country. And it kept the stubborn ones from losing confidence in the drilling.

There was scarcely a day when they did not make some small raid either against the fort or upon one of the wagon trains along the trail. Never before had Indians been known to fight in this strategic way. In the old days they had struck, then fled the scene.

Their tepees stretched far up the Little Goose River with more Indians coming in constantly. Crazy Horse and Red Cloud were determined to keep their people together and to harry the soldiers at the fort until they left the country.

But still the wood choppers' axes hacked away and the hammers banged. Peace and quiet had fled from the Powder River country. No wonder the besieged soldiers called their site Fort Perilous, although it had been given the name of Fort Phil Kearny. Crazy Horse saw to it that the soldiers could not go a mile from the fort without being attacked. In the middle of the month of Cherries Reddening, he led a small band close enough to the troops to run off a large string of mules, besides killing two men and wounding three others who set out in pursuit.

Every night the campfires blazed along the hills and streams; the war drums throbbed incessantly and any time of day or night wild war whoops echoed from hill to hill to remind those within the fort of an enemy who never slept.

The Sioux lodges stretched so far up the Little Goose that it took a full circle of the sun to ride their length. And under Crazy Horse's drilling the young men were learning to fight in a unit. Time and again they practiced their new tactics on the wood trains which must travel seven miles to hew the logs used in building the palisades of the fort. Always the trains traveled under heavy soldier escort and it was rare good fun to send the wood cutters and soldiers scooting back to the fort under a shower of arrows.

A news runner came galloping into the Oglala camp one evening with word that a train of reinforcements of soldiers was marching toward the fort on the Piney. With them was a young chief who called himself Captain Fetterman. The Loafers-Around-the-Fort Indians had heard him make his big brags.

The news runner reported that Fetterman had boasted, "Give me eighty men and I will ride through the whole Sioux nation."

Crazy Horse's eyes had gleamed when he heard this news. "I hope the young chief Fetterman gets his eighty men soon," he said. "We will see how fast he rides through the Sioux nation."

If Carrington expected the Sioux to withdraw to their camps as was the usual Indian custom with the coming of winter he was to be disappointed.

"We will stay and fight until the soldiers leave our land or are all killed," Crazy Horse told his followers.

During the time of the Sun Dance, the soldiers had a spell of comparative peace. Later many of the Indian men left on a hunt for winter meat, but Crazy Horse persuaded enough warriors to stay to make life miserable for the soldiers cooped within "Fort Perilous."

It was early in the Middle of the Winter Moon, when Crazy Horse led a band of warriors to attack the wood cutters' train two miles from the fort on Pilot Hill. The white men made a square corral of their wagons and banged away at the Indians who circled the wagons, shooting arrows when making sudden dashes in close to the corral. Crazy Horse watching the maneuvers and giving signals from a hilltop, was well pleased with the way things were going. His young men were learning their lesson; fighting the way he was teaching them. As he had expected, soon the soldiers came pouring from the fort.

Crazy Horse put his eagle-wing whistle to his lips and blew a signal. Would his plan work? He had ordered Hump, American Horse, He Dog and Touch-the-Clouds to conceal themselves in the ravines beside the valley. At his whistle they rode out and he galloped to meet them. The other Sioux raced away, as had been planned, as though trying to get away from the oncoming soldiers, leaving Crazy Horse and his four friends behind. It appeared that their horses were too slow to make much headway. On, on the horse soldiers came, almost catching up with them, but not quite. Then suddenly several yelling Sioux jumped from behind the bushes, firing at the soldiers who turned and fled. Crazy Horse gave the whistle signal for all of his warriors to join the pursuit. But it was too late, for Carrington with his sword flashing in the sun rode out at the head of a rescue detachment from the fort. The Sioux, outnumbered, were forced to withdraw.

Crazy Horse found words coming easily to his lips that night as he harangued his warriors. "Will you never learn?" he shouted. "Again you foolish ones spoiled a perfect surround by being too eager for personal glory. We have but two scalps when we should have the scalps of every man in Fetterman's command."

Never had the Sioux warriors taken such a tongue lashing. All their people frowned upon them. The old way of counting coup was not popular now. If they were driven from the Powder River country, where would they go? The buffalo and game were gone from the plains. The white men were pushing into the Black Hills for gold. There was no other sanctuary left for them. At last the Sioux realized this was to be a grim fight to the finish. Crazy Horse with his incessant ranting was right. The white man's way of fighting was best. If he was to be driven out, they must beat him in his own way. There was no scalp dance that night. The warriors who had spoiled the surround sought their tepees with hanging heads.

The Sioux bided their time for half a moon. The snow was thin on the hills, but the sun was bright, making the snow gleam and sparkle. Crazy Horse, in war dress, sat on a hilltop glowering down upon the fort. The palisade wall was finished. Within its confines most of the buildings must be nearly completed. Without the wood train to heckle, it would be difficult to keep his young men from being bored. They would want to be off to the hills to hunt or to steal ponies from the Crows, or when it got colder, to stay snugly in their warm tepees. And the soldiers would be safe inside their fortress walls once they bristled with big guns.

Crazy Horse heard the bugle blow within the walls of the fort stockade. He was learning the meaning of the bugle calls. Soon the wood train rode out escorted by a strong detachment of soldiers. The young Shirt Wearer straightened up on his horse and a wide grin crossed his usually serious features. He recognized that man who rode so jauntily at the head of the column. It was the one called

Fetterman — he who had boasted, "Give me eighty men and I'll ride through the Sioux nation." Now he had that many.

Answering his signal a group of warriors joined him to attack the wood train. They were his picked men — the other Shirt Wearers and the special warrior each had chosen.

"You will hide in this draw," Crazy Horse directed. "Watch for my signals."

He rode to a higher spot where he could watch what was going on. There was commotion in the camps. His signals had been seen, and were being relayed to the rest of the warriors.

His men were catching their horses and were riding out as had been planned so many times. He turned his horse back into the valley to meet the Shirt Wearers and to lead them forth.

Riding at their head, Crazy Horse blinked, hardly able to believe his eyes. Coming over Lodge Trail Ridge was the one called Fetterman with his eighty men. Crazy Horse whirled his horse and his followers whirled too, appearing to be trying to get away from the soldiers who were not far behind. They sawed their arms up and down, pretending to whip their horses, all the while holding them back.

On, on the soldiers came riding fast. Crazy Horse threw anxious glances over his shoulder, appearing to be frightened. And he was. Frightened that some of his reckless young men could not wait, but would come dashing out and spoil another surround. But none was in sight. When he and his small group reached the ravines which opened out on each side of the valley, triumphantly he raised his arm in the signal to attack. From the ravines the Sioux

came pouring like flood waters and those who had been hiding in the grass at the end of the valley leaped to their feet and came rushing.

It was all over in a short time. The Indians fought with their own weapons, arrows, war clubs and lances. Two or three had old muzzle loaders, but no ammunition. Yet the eighty soldiers with their firearms were no match for the fury of the Sioux fighting to keep their hunting ground. Fetterman and his eighty soldiers lay slain to the last man.

ABANDON
OUR
LAND!

■■■■■■■■ 17

MORE SOLDIERS with wagon guns appeared at the top of Lodge Trail Ridge. The Indians, busy in the valley below scalping and robbing the bodies, dared the Blue Coats to come down and fight but the invitation was not accepted. Crazy Horse and his warriors, too, had had enough of fighting for one day. The soldiers disappeared from the ridge and the Indians went back to their lodges, to huddle close to their campfires for it had turned bitter cold.

Hoye! The name of Crazy Horse was great among his people this day. His plan had worked. For the first time a decoy had been carried through to completion without any rash young men's rushing forth to spoil it. Because of his clever strategy, every man in the brave Fetterman's command had been killed — even he, the bold one who had bragged that with eighty men he would ride through the Sioux nation! Never had the white men suffered such a defeat. In every tepee that afternoon the name of Crazy

Horse was being said in praise. Once Hump had predicted that Crazy Horse would be the greatest warrior among the whole Lakota nation. Hump himself was still great, but truly had he spoken, for now Crazy Horse was the greatest of them all, even though he was only twenty-two snows old.

Crazy Horse sat in his tepee more quiet than usual. He was thinking about the brave white chief Fetterman. It was sad that such a brave man had to die, yet the whites should know that they could not drive the Indians from their own country. How good it was that his warriors had got so many firearms and some ammunition — things they sorely needed. He rather dreaded appearing at the victory dance tonight, for he knew that he would be spoken of loudly and pushed to the front. For such things he had no liking. He considered staying in his tepee, but a leader was expected to appear before the people on occasions like this.

But no victory dance was held that night. The temperature dropped to the coldest within the memory of the older Crazy Horse and a raging blizzard came up. The Indians were glad to huddle over the campfires in their snug tepees. The victory dance would have to wait until the weather cleared. So would the attack on the fort which Crazy Horse had planned. He knew that with the wiping out of Fetterman's entire command, the forces at the fort must be greatly weakened. Now was the time to strike before reinforcements could be sent from Fort Laramie.

No attack was possible, though, until the weather moderated. Men would freeze in such a storm. But there was no hurry. The storm would hold up Carrington, too. He could not send for reinforcements until it abated.

Little did Crazy Horse or his people dream that at that very moment a brave young man known as "Portugee" Phillips on a fine horse was floundering through the snow drifts on his way to Fort Laramie to tell of the Fetterman

tragedy and to ask for immediate reinforcements. By the time Crazy Horse was ready to attack the fort, new troops had arrived. It was too late!

The long, bitter winter dragged like a lingering sickness. There was no big fighting although Crazy Horse and Red Cloud sent bands of warriors out upon frequent raids, to fire flaming arrows into the fort and to attack any wagon train which ventured forth.

But trouble developed among the Sioux. The young men were becoming bored. The Indians did not like staying in one large camp; it was their custom to break up into small camps during the winter. Too, there was jealousy in their ranks. Man-Afraid had been the great one among the Sioux; now Crazy Horse and Red Cloud were the ones who were praised as the big men.

There were some who sought to drag Crazy Horse down from the high place to which he had climbed. No Water was the noisiest of these trouble makers. "Has-ka would have you fight in the white man's manner," he told the young warriors, "because he is afraid you will earn honors which will put you above him." Many who preferred the old way of fighting were ready to believe this. No Water had achieved no prominence as a warrior, but as grandson of the great chief Old Smoke, he was looked up to and because his voice was strong he still had a following.

Spring finally came to the Powder River country. The ponies fattened on the rich grass. The Sioux continued to harass the soldiers at the fort on the Piney all through the summer. Crazy Horse had been riding far and wide carrying the war pipe to bring the tribes which had wandered away back to the camp near the hated fort. Slowly band by band they gathered until the smoke from a thousand or

more lodges again twirled lazily toward the clouds. *Hoye!*
It was good to see their numbers so strong.

A few moons later, Crazy Horse planned to strike again,
hoping to repeat the Fetterman victory. A crew of wood-
choppers was sent out from the fort under soldier escort.
The soldier chief must have expected trouble, for after he
had sent a detail to the woods he had his men take the
boxes from the wood-hauling wagons and form a corral of
them within which they placed their supplies.

Crazy Horse and a band of his painted braves mounted
on their fastest ponies, hid in a draw, then rushed to attack
the woodsmen when they were well out in the open. Four
of them were slain; the others fled to the wagon box corral
squatting on the open space.

For a time all was silent within the wagon box corral.
The Indians could see that blankets had been thrown over
the tops of the wagons and between them were sacks, probably of grain, together with the oxen yokes, chains, and
other implements.

Crazy Horse glanced over his shoulder at his braves.
Never had he seen so many in one band. They would make
short work of the whites hiding within their silly wagon
box corral. He had no idea how many soldiers and wood-
choppers there were, but no matter. His force was like the
leaves on the summer trees in number. And they had the
Fetterman guns, making them stronger than they had ever
been before.

Crazy Horse whirled his blanket over his head, a signal
for attack. Slapping their mouths in war whoop the warriors galloped forward. This time there was no decoy strategy; it was proper action for the young men to swoop upon
the enemy in an attempt to be first to count coup. When
just beyond range of rifle fire of the soldiers the Sioux

started circling. They expected a volley of rifle fire, then a pause while the soldiers reloaded. The plan was that during that pause the Sioux would rush in.

Crazy Horse drew his spotted horse to its haunches, amazed at what he saw. The first expected volley came, but following it was no pause for reloading; instead there was no letup from the guns. Crazy Horse gave the blanket signal for his warriors to continue circling. His men rained arrows within the fortress and those who had guns used them, but that murderous fire from every angle of the fortress blazed unceasingly at the Indians. Bewildered, Crazy Horse signaled for retreat of his warriors to a clump of trees for a powwow.

The pocket mirrors of the lookouts began flashing from the hilltops, calling more warriors to the battle in which the Indians were beginning to believe themselves outnumbered.

Now Crazy Horse sent those of his men who had guns creeping forward through the tall grass close to the wagon boxes. They blazed away at the corral until the boxes were riddled by bullets, but there was no way of telling whether or not anyone inside was being injured. The white men had ceased to fire except when an Indian raised his head.

Other warriors began to arrive. Crazy Horse decided that the silence within the corral meant that most of the white men had been killed. Forming his warriors into a huge wedge he advanced in a mass attack. Again came that terrible and continuous spray of death in their faces. But still they pushed forward. Surely the soldiers' rifles would empty and during the pause while they reloaded the Indians could swarm over the wagon boxes and swiftly clean out the nest within. But the fire never ceased, and the Sioux ranks broke. Crazy Horse again led his braves forth on horseback, but once more that withering fire drove them back.

Now the sun was nearing the edge of the world. Crazy Horse spread his hands in the signal for his warriors to scatter to their camps; the fighting was done for the day.

His head sank on his chest as he slumped beside his family campfire. He shook his head as his mother handed him a spoonful of stew. He could not eat. His heart was sick with the defeat. How could the Sioux ever hope to drive the Blue Coats from their hunting grounds? The white men had some new sort of rapid-fire guns and his heart was heavy with discouragement when he thought of their own puny weapons — bows and arrows and the eighty guns taken from the Fetterman Blue Coats — guns for which there was insufficient ammunition.

In the days that followed, it was as he had feared — many of his warriors showed that they had lost faith in him. His medicine which had heretofore been so strong had failed in the fight against the wagon boxes. Many of his warriors left the camp to scatter and go hunting. He had a difficult time keeping enough of them together to harass those at the fort and to block travel over the Bozeman Trail.

Another snow passed and another spring came, with Crazy Horse still grimly holding his small forces together around the hated fort.

One day when the plum trees were in bloom five messengers rode into the Oglala camp and asked the head men to meet them in council. "The Great Father has sent piles of gifts so high," the spokesman said, holding his hand above his head. "Come in to the fort and sign the peace paper and all of those gifts will be yours." Crazy Horse rose to his feet deliberately, and the atmosphere within the council tepee seemed to crackle with the force emanated from him. "We will put our hands to the pen on the white man's paper on our own terms only," he roared. "The Blue Coats will go away. From all of the forts along the Bozeman Trail. The white men must leave our hunting grounds forever. The Powder River country and the Black Hills must be OURS."

The "*haus*" of agreement were loud. No one argued for accepting the presents of the White Father. All were united on Crazy Horse's stand.

There were other powwows of the same sort, but influenced by Crazy Horse, the Sioux remained firm in their decision until at last, for the first time in history, American troops bowed to the will of the Red Man.

On a golden day in the Moon of Plums Ripening, Crazy Horse and his people stood on a near-by hillside and watched the Blue Coats haul down their bright-colored cloth with the corner of stars and the red and white stripes. Then the soldiers marched in a column from Fort Phil Kearny back toward Fort Laramie. The fort had been abandoned.

Such a roar of triumph came from the throats of his people as Crazy Horse had never heard. Then they swooped upon the fort. The Indian women followed chattering like magpies as they swarmed into the buildings.

"It will be fine and warm to live in white man houses," they cried. "More comfortable than our tepees."

An angry roar came from the throat of Crazy Horse when he heard such talk. "We will not become as white men," he cried. "Living in houses would make our men soft. Put the torch to the buildings!"

While the women wailed their disappointment his men obeyed his order. As the black smoke billowed upward, it seemed to make clean again the air and quiet peace came

once more to the Powder River country. Again it belonged to the Indians who would die rather than give it up.

Slowly Crazy Horse walked to a lonely hilltop where he spread out his arms and sent up his thanks to the *Wakan Tanka* for this great victory. The Holy Mystery had given him the power and the plan to lead the Lakotas to this triumph. In his heart was humble gratitude for the service he had been able to perform for his people.

TROUBLE
AMONG
THE
OGLALAS
........18

AFTER THE BLUE COATS had been removed from the
Hated Fort on the Piney there was to be a new treaty giving
back the Sioux their own land. Because Red Cloud made
a loud noise with his tongue in all of the councils, the white
men regarded him as a chief and asked that he come to
Laramie to sign the paper. He was not a chief, so all of
the different bands of Lakotas — the Oglalas, the Brulés,
the Hunkpapas, had to gather in council to make him what
they called a "Treaty Chief." This was different from being
an actual chief. Red Cloud was pleased and flattered by
the honor, as he had always been one who strove hard for
power.

"So long as the grass shall grow, so long as the rivers
flow," the new treaty said the Sioux could hold the Powder
River country. Many of the bands gathered for feasting

and dancing in celebration because the soldier chiefs had been so generous.

"They only give us back what is our own," Crazy Horse said scornfully.

He had been keeping out of Red Cloud's way ever since the Fetterman and the Wagon Box fights, for during the siege against the whites he had been gaining such prominence that he put Red Cloud in the background — something which the older warrior could not endure. Rivalry between the two had been smouldering ever since Red Cloud had not been chosen a Shirt Wearer.

Now Crazy Horse had to endure the humiliating sight of the older warrior's strutting around as if he alone were responsible for this latest and greatest victory over the whites.

A messenger came from the fort inviting the most prominent Oglalas to go to Washington to visit the Great Father. Before it could be decided in council, Red Cloud was the first to say he would go. It disgusted Crazy Horse that one of their head men should be so eager to run after white man presents. He was afraid that under the influence of the white men's flattery Red Cloud might be persuaded to sign away the rights of their people. Yet Red Cloud could not be dissuaded from going. It was whispered in the Oglala camp that he had hopes that the Great Father would make him a great chief over all the Sioux.

Crazy Horse turned away when he heard such talk. He would not speak against his rival, but he wondered why any man should strive for such an empty honor. It would be a fine thing to be made a chief by one's own people, but to have the Great White Father say an Indian was a chief made that man ridiculous.

Red Cloud accompanied by nineteen other Oglalas went

to Washington. Crazy Horse was asked by his people to go, but he chose to remain with his band. The Crows had come raiding lately and had driven off a number of ponies. His people begged him to get up a big war party to fight them. Before they set out, the old men of the Oglalas came from the council lodge, bearing the two sacred lances which, it was said, had been in the tribe since the beginning of time. They were lances given by the *Wakan Tanka* to make the people strong. Crazy Horse had never seen the lances, which had been kept in the lodge of Wild Fox, the oldest holy man of the Oglalas, but around campfires he had heard tales about them — how they were to be hidden until two men should rise among the people strong enough and wise enough to be entrusted with their keeping.

As the group of warriors led by Crazy Horse and He Dog rode slowly through the camp, the old men approached them and the riders checked their horses. The old men solemnly extended the lances and Crazy Horse and He Dog as solemnly accepted them while Wild Fox said, "These we give to you — our two young men who try only to keep our people strong. We entrust you with these lances so that power will remain with us as long as the sun shall shine."

Even though surprised by this great honor, Crazy Horse maintained his dignity as he bowed his thanks. This was beyond his farthest dreams. During his lifetime and the lifetime of his father no one had been deemed worthy of such an honor. A feeling of power surged through him as he rode forth with a lance proudly held before him. The people following from the village shouted their joy that two young men among them had been found worthy of being Lance Bearers — an even greater distinction than that of being a Shirt Wearer.

After riding for nearly half the journey of the sun across

the sky, the scouts who had been sent out in advance of the war party gave the blanket signal that the Crow village had been sighted. The war party hid behind rocks to don war regalia and paint, then rode to the top of a hill overlooking the Crow camp stretched along a valley on the Little Big Horn River. Raising his lance in the signal for attack, Crazy Horse with He Dog at his side galloped the full length of the enemy camp. Arrows showered about them, but so strong was their medicine that they were unharmed. Seeing that the medicine of the Sioux leaders was so good, the Crows became demoralized and fled for the hills. The Oglalas took some scalps and many horses; enough for them to consider the raid a success.

Hoye! It was good to have the white men gone and to be doing Indian things again. That night when the warriors returned there was a big victory dance around the scalps as in the old days, with Crazy Horse and He Dog in the center of the circle holding the lances. Both had donned their fine buckskin shirts with the painting of their coups — the garments which only the Shirt Wearers were permitted to wear. As he stood there with all eyes upon him — some admiring, some envious, the set-apart feeling he had as a boy returned to his thoughts. Now he was truly set apart — but in a different way. His wish for greatness had come true — far beyond his ambitions.

When he was younger he had looked forward to a moment like this as the crowning goal of a lifetime. But his ambition had been pushed forward to a far greater objective. Personal glory was fine. But now that he had its mantle on his shoulders, it was not enough. He must use his medicine for the good of his people. He would never be content until they were safe — until the whites were driven from the land of the Lakotas.

His thoughts still seething with his plans, he strode toward his tepee. Nearing it he was surprised to see the glow of firelight shining through the skins. What could it be? Who was in his lodge? He lifted the flap and peered inside, then stepped back startled. It couldn't be — he peered inside again. Yes — his eyes were not deceiving him. It was actually Hopa in a snow-white deerskin dress, kneeling beside the fire stirring the pot of stew just as if she belonged there.

He stood there, still holding the flap of the tepee, blinking, his features questioning.

"The stew is ready," she said, holding out the big horn spoon to him.

When he had recovered from his surprise he asked gently, "Why are you here?"

She stood up, folded her hands before her and looked down at them.

"A Lakota woman is privileged to leave the lodge of her husband," she reminded him. "No one can stop her. It was always you whose moccasins I wished to make. My father gave me to No Water because of his many horses and because he was then great among us."

Crazy Horse's eyes gleamed in the firelight. "So now that I have become great among the Oglalas you leave the man who is little." There was a note of irony in his voice. But she chose to ignore it and lifting her eyes to his in a soft, pleading voice she sang,

> *Many are the warriors, many warriors,*
> *You alone are he who pleases me.*
> *Over all I love thee.*
> *Long shall be the years of parting!*

As the tender words fell upon his ears, all of his doubts dropped away. He stepped to her side and gently lifting her blanket from her shoulders, he wrapped it about both of them.

Strange how all of his dreams were coming true at once. He had been honored above all of his people by being made a Shirt Wearer and a Lance Carrier. Often he had imagined seeing Hopa beside his campfire stirring the stew, or, holding her in his arms. But always he had put the picture out of his mind. Now this dream, too, had come true.

There was a noise outside the tepee, then, "Ah-hhh! There he is. The man who steals his friend's wife!" An angry voice jarred Crazy Horse back to earth.

He dropped the blanket and whirled to face No Water who had flung open the skins and stood at the entrance of the tepee with a leveled revolver in his hand. The gun blazed. Pain seared Crazy Horse's cheek and crashed through his head. Blackness descended.

When he came alive again the medicine man was prancing up and down beside his pallet and shaking his rattle. Crazy Horse looked around. He Dog rose from the sleeping robes, came across the tepee and stood over him.

"She is gone to her relatives," he said in answer to the question in his friend's eyes.

"Then — she is unharmed?" with painful difficulty Crazy Horse got the words past his sore and swollen mouth.

He Dog nodded.

Crazy Horse lifted an exploring hand. It felt as if the bullet had torn half his face away and there was a hole in the lower part of the back of his head where the bullet had come out. The pain made him sick, but he was relieved to find that the entire side of his face had not been blasted away. Everything in the tepee — He Dog, the medicine

man, all swayed crazily. But upon hearing that Hopa was unharmed he lay back and dizziness picked him up and swept him away again.

He did not know how many sleeps had passed before the searing heat in the wound and the dizziness left him, but one day he opened his eyes and things stayed in their place as they should. Seeing him stir, He Dog came to sit beside him.

"It is good to see you well again, my friend," he said. "There have been bad things going on in our camp. Now that you will get well, matters will right themselves."

"What bad things?" Crazy Horse asked weakly.

"Our people feared you, their great man, would die," He Dog said. "There are those who would go out to kill

No Water. And there are those of his friends who said that he did right to try to kill you."

"Our camp divided — over me!" Crazy Horse groaned.

"It was so," He Dog admitted. "For a time it looked as if there would be war among our own people. Then the woman, to keep our people from trouble, went back to No Water. No Water took her and went to another camp. So the trouble is ended."

The time of the Sun Dance had come when Crazy Horse was able to move around on shaky legs again. His cheek bore the jagged scar he would have for the rest of his life. Then it was that the Big Bellies met and later they summoned Crazy Horse. He went to them carrying his white buckskin shirt in its embroidered case. This, without a word, he laid at the feet of the Big Bellies. He, who had sworn an oath to protect his people when the shirt was put upon him, had been the cause of trouble among them.

Then, between two lines of curious watchers who had come to see what was going on, he stalked from the council lodge, head high, eyes straight ahead. How short a time ago there seemed no end to good things happening for him. Now suddenly everything was going the other way.

The day after Crazy Horse's shirt had been taken away, a hunting party, their faces daubed with dirt as the sign of mourning, came in making the "Ey-ee" of sorrow. They brought the news to the tepee of Crazy Horse's father that his son, Little Hawk, had been killed by white men digging for yellow dirt.

Crazy Horse with a stony look upon his face sat by the fire listening as this bad thing was told by the hunters. Here was another crime added to the many done by the white men. Was there never to be any end to it? "So long as the grass shall grow" the Sioux were to have this land.

But now the white men had come prowling — digging in the earth, killing! Killing! Killing! The brave Little Hawk, his own brother was dead! All because of the white men's greed for the yellow dirt — and because they did not keep the treaty. Hate like poison surged through Crazy Horse's veins.

He got on his horse and rode out alone, through the country where the gold-crazed miners were, and brought back the body of his brother to place it on the burial scaffold.

WE
WILL NOT
SELL
PA
SAPA

■■■■■■■ 19

T HE WOUND in Crazy Horse's face healed, but the soreness
he carried within his heart from being unshirted was long
in mending.

Was this his punishment for allowing his personal ambition to rise above his more lofty aim of saving his people?
Yet the greater aim was still burning in his heart. Now,
though, it would be more difficult to accomplish because
he had lost face.

He knew that his disgrace had been brought about by his
enemies within the band who wished to pull him down
from the high place he had earned. His enemies were not
only against him, but there were those who stood for the
white man's ways even though those ways were not for
the good of the people. Once more he felt as he had so
often when a boy — as if every hand were raised against
him. The humiliation of having been torn down from the

high place was worse than if he had never been given it. But no matter what happened to him, he knew that he had been good for the people.

There was one, though, who was not against him. Her-Black-Robe let him know by certain shy glances that she still thought him the greatest warrior among the Oglalas. Won by her faithfulness, Crazy Horse put Hopa from his heart forever and took as his wife this one who had long been yearning for him.

Red Cloud came back from his visit to the Great Father in Washington talking big of the things he had seen. He had returned to camp with several pack horses laden with presents. There were many presents for the rest of the tribes, too, he said, if they would go to Laramie to receive them.

"What was in the treaty you signed?" Crazy Horse asked him. "Did you tell them that you were the big man among the Lakotas and did you sign away our land?"

Red Cloud's eyes hardened. "Our people can roam this land that the Great Father gave us," he said. "But no traders can come to us until we go onto a reservation."

"A reservation? What is that?" Crazy Horse asked.

Others had come close to hear what was being said.

"A reservation is a big place the White Father sets aside just for the Indians," Red Cloud replied. "There will be food for us and many presents." His eyes wavered and he dropped his glance. "The white men are too strong to go against," he went on lamely.

"You have turned into a white man," Crazy Horse spat out the words. He turned and strode away, too disgusted to talk longer.

He went to the tepee of Hump, the warrior. After they had discussed Red Cloud's actions, Hump, seeing the dis-

couragement on his friend's face, said, "The Snakes, our
enemies, are camping too close to our camping ground.
Shall we drive them away?" Crazy Horse was eager for the
raid.

They organized a small party, got their guns and bows
and as soon as they came within sight of the camp, they
rushed to attack, but most of the enemy had guns whereas
the Oglalas had only four firearms in their entire party.
The battle was a short one ending in retreat with Hump
and Crazy Horse riding in the rear to protect the rest.
Before they reached a safe distance, Hump fell forward on
his horse's neck with a bullet through his head. Instantly
Crazy Horse clutched the body and dragged it across his
horse, determined that the enemy should not take the scalp
of the warrior who had meant so much to him all his life.

Rain began to fall as the defeated party entered the village. With his own hands Crazy Horse erected the burial
scaffold, then as he and young Hump lifted the body of his
friend upon it, it seemed that the sun would never shine
for him again.

The long cold winter passed. Spring came and with it a
little daughter for Crazy Horse. They-Are-Afraid-of-Her he
called the child, for he was sure that because of the fine
deeds she would perform all people would stand in awe of
her.

The buffalo, which heretofore returned with the coming
of the grass, did not return except in small bunches. The
memory of the old days when it took several suns for one
herd to pass were as a dream. Now hard hunting was re-
quired to keep the camp supplied with meat and often the
parfleches were flat and the hides to be made into robes,
tepees and the multitude of things the Indians used were
scarce.

Some of the women and the old men grumbled about the state of affairs. "Red Cloud sends word that on the reservation there is plenty of everything," they pointed out.

"Spotted Tail seems content on the reservation named for him," others chimed in. "There he is strong in the power the white men have put in his hands. His people are not in need."

"We are Oglalas," Crazy Horse cried in a firm voice. "The bravest and strongest of the Lakota tribes. We will not bow to the will of the white man. We will live as the *Wakan Tanka* intended. If we keep to the old ways of our fathers the buffalo will come back. It is because some of us have taken up the bad ways of the whites that the herds have disappeared."

It pleased him to see some of the doubts and dissatisfactions ease from his tribesmen's faces as he talked. His medicine with them was still strong even though he had been unshirted. There might be a chance for him yet to save them and lead them to final peace — if they would heed him and follow his counsel.

When the buffalo herds returned again his people would see that the ways of their fathers were best. Then those who had been softened by the white men's ways would lose their influence. He, Crazy Horse, must exert himself still harder to lead his people to eventual victory.

He set a time for his people to hold the buffalo dance. They donned buffalo robes, with the skin of the head left on and pranced around to the beat of the drums until they were exhausted. But when the hunters went out to search for the herds, they were not to be found. They saw something else, however, which filled their hearts with alarm. They found a band of white men accompanied by soldiers, measuring the ground for the iron road to carry their fire engine straight through the Indians' hunting ground. The soldier chief of this party was the one called Yellow Hair, Custer, the one the news rider said had pursued the Cheyennes all over the Republican River Valley and who had slaughtered the friendly Indians in Black Kettle's village on the Washita. Already the hearts of the Oglalas were hot with hate against this new enemy.

"It is as I told you all along," Crazy Horse repeated. "We must hold our hunting grounds from the whites. We must drive them away or we will die."

There was fighting from day to day, with the yellow-haired chief chasing the Sioux and Cheyennes across the Yellowstone River. The Indians did not have enough guns to do much harm to the heavily-guarded surveying party; all that they could do was to follow like a pack of wolves and pick off a stray man now and then or drive off their horses whenever they could sneak in among them.

Crazy Horse led the fighting, but other things weighed on his mind. Her-Black-Robe lay in the tepee wasting away with the white man's coughing sickness and the child, They-Are-Afraid-of-Her, was like a delicate flower meant to bloom for only a short time. It made the hearts of the Oglalas soft to see their great warrior walk through the camp carrying the little girl on his shoulders. She was fair of skin and hair like her father and there was a sweetness and fragility about her that was very appealing.

Another winter came, with heavy snows, much cold and the game driven far away. The buffalo were scarce and there were many lean bellies in camp. The men grumbled that they needed more guns and powder. Red Cloud said that the white men had promised many guns to his people if he took them on the reservation.

"Red Cloud! Phaugh!" Crazy Horse cried, his eyes

snapping. "He is like long hid away from the sun — pale and soft. He should know by this time how little the white man's promises mean!"

Now Crazy Horse could not carry They-Are-Afraid-of-Her through the village for she lay gasping, choking with a new sickness brought to the Oglala camp by a trader's son. A sickness which made the throat close shut. Before he went

out to find meat, Crazy Horse called the medicine man to
frighten away the evil spirits from his daughter's wasting
body. When he returned he found Her-Black-Robe sitting
on the ground inside the tepee holding their child in her
arms, rocking back and forth and moaning. Her stricken
face told him what had happened. Gently he took the cold
body from her arms, wrapped it in the best robe in the
tepee. He gathered up her doll made of deerskin, her small
drum, a willow circle from which dangled bright feathers,
stones and seeds. These he placed with her on a scaffold and
shot his best horse to put beneath for her to ride in comfort
to the *Wakan Tanka*. Then he climbed up beside her and
for three suns and darknesses lay clasping the body in his
arms.

When he turned away from the scaffold it was as though
he had died, too. His stumbling feet carried him to the
tepee, but his body felt like an empty, worn out parfleche.
He was devoid of every sensation, every thought, save
anguish.

But Crazy Horse was not allowed long to brood over his
grief. The bad things which were happening to his people
once more demanded his attention. Yellow Hair had led
a band of Blue Coats into the Black Hills, the sacred land
of the Sioux. There they were cutting a road past Bear
Butte, the place where the Lakota councils had been held
as long as man could remember.

The Indians called Yellow Hair's trail the Thieves' Road.
Fury raged in the blood of every Lakota that their sacred
Black Hills had been desecrated by the white men. But that
was not all. The soldiers had come across a handful of
Oglala hunters and killed several and wounded others. Some,
hearing of Yellow Hair's approach, had fled leaving their

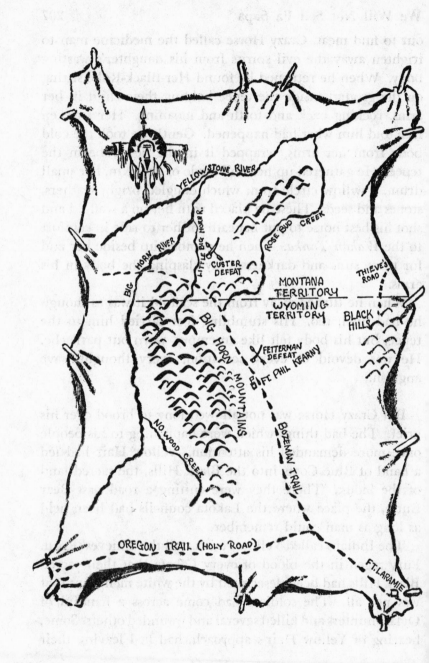

hunters without protection. This was a shameful thing to have happened. Custer had marched into their sacred land and out again without so much as an arrow's being fired at him. But what could the Indians do with only a few old guns and little powder, when the soldiers had wagonloads of firearms and ammunition?

Worst of all, word came from the fort that Custer was saying that he had found gold in the Black Hills. Much gold. It could be picked up from the grass roots.

"Ah-hhh!" Crazy Horse moaned at this news. He knew what gold did to the white men. Now they would come in swarms, like wild men, fighting, clawing, killing — not only the Indians, but each other. He wondered what there was about the yellow metal that turned men into fiends. One could not even eat the stuff, and elk teeth, eagle claws or even feathers made more attractive adornments.

Sure enough, it was not long before the white men began streaming into the Black Hills, frightening away the game — digging holes, rocking water and gravel from the streams back and forth in their little pans.

The new happenings were bad, but they had one good consequence; they united the Oglalas who had been bickering among themselves because of the hard times. Some had wanted to go to the reservation for the white man's gifts and others had wanted to heed Crazy Horse's advice to hold to the old way of life.

Now they came clamoring to him for leadership.

"The *Wakan Tanka* gave us the land and the herds for our own," he told the people, and with his words strength flowed from him into them. "Even the White Father in Washington promised us the Black Hills and the Powder River country so long as the grass shall grow, so long as the streams shall flow. Already that promise is broken. But the land is ours. We will not be driven away. We must fight for what is ours."

His people nodded in agreement. "We will fight," they cried. "The medicine of Crazy Horse is strong. With him to lead us we will drive the whites from our land. Soon life for us will be good again!"

A new recklessness possessed Crazy Horse since the death of his daughter. There was a wild look in his eyes which made men fear him and there was new power in him, too, which at the same time drew men to him for leadership. There was little they could do, however, save make raids upon small parties of miners.

"We must have guns! We must have guns!" Crazy Horse shouted over and over again. The main object now of most raids was to obtain guns and ammunition.

But it seemed as if there was no stemming the flood of humanity that the word "gold" had unleashed. Red Cloud and some of his chiefs again went to Washington to try to persuade the Great Father to take the white men from their country. However, no sooner were they out of the way than a large band of miners, protected by soldiers, entered the Black Hills.

A-hhh! So this was the way it was to be. The Great Father promised them the land "so long as the grass shall grow" then turned right around and gave soldier protection to those bent upon stealing the country from the Indians.

Crazy Horse and his people were not surprised when Red Cloud came back from Washington with word that the chiefs of many other bands had also been called there and the Great Father and his head men had tried to coax them to sell the Black Hills.

"Sell the Black Hills!" The cry ran through the camp. What else should Red Cloud expect! He had been so loaded with presents that it was a wonder he had not touched his hand to the stick to make black marks on the paper.

Now the Great Father was sending peace men to all of the agencies with huge wagonloads of presents to bribe the chiefs into selling the Black Hills.

"How can any people sell land?" Crazy Horse asked when he heard this news. "Land is something the *Wakan Tanka* gave us for our needs, just as He gave us the air and the water and the animals. Even if we should sell the sacred land of our fathers for what the white man calls money, what would we do with the green paper? Money is no use to us."

"We could trade the money for guns to kill the white men who steal the country from us," He Dog growled.

There were those among the Oglalas, however, whose hearts and minds had been bought by the white men's gifts and promises. These boughten ones talked loud for the sale of the Black Hills. The Blue Coats called such Sioux "good" Indians; the others were "hostiles."

Now and then Crazy Horse sent some of his braves to swoop down upon the agencies to keep the "good" chiefs reminded that there would be trouble if *Pa Sapa* were sold.

The white chiefs announced that a council would be held at the place called Lone Tree, between the Red Cloud and the Spotted Tail reservations. The tribes came from all directions and tepees sprang up on the hillsides like mushrooms and the valleys were dark with Indian ponies.

The white chiefs sat on their little canvas chairs, their soldiers behind them, while the Sioux chiefs sat cross-legged on the ground in a circle before the white chiefs. Silently a great circle of dark scowling faces built up a wall beyond them.

The white man called Brunot got to his feet and bowed his head to offer up a prayer asking the blessing and guidance of the white chief's God.

When he sat down Red Cloud leapt to his feet and holding his arms aloft he cried, "No! No! The white man has prayed to the Great Spirit that the Indians' hearts be made good for what is to happen here. Now the red man will pray to Him for His help:

"O Great Spirit! I pray to You to look at us. We are Your children and You placed us first in this land. We pray You to look down upon us so that nothing but the truth shall be spoken in this council. We do not ask for anything but what is right and just. You made Your red children, O Great Spirit, You must have mercy upon them. Now we are before You today praying You to look down on us and take pity upon Your poor red children. I pray You to have nothing but truth spoken here. You are the protector of the people born with bows and arrows as well as the people born with hats and garments and I hope we don't pray to You in vain. We are poor and ignorant. Our fathers told us we would not be in misery if we would ask Your assistance. O Great Spirit, look down on Your red children and take pity upon them!"

Crazy Horse nodded his approval when Red Cloud sat down. He had felt contempt of the former great man because he had been so easily bought, but his prayer sounded sincere and humble. He must still have the interests of his people at heart.

For three suns there was much talk but no results — no decisions. At the first sundown Crazy Horse withdrew his warriors into the hills. There were hotheaded ones among them who were all for riding in and killing the white commissioners now before the bad thing could be done.

"It is not the time," Crazy Horse spoke sternly. Then he told them of his plan for preventing the sale of the Black Hills, and without drawing the fire of all the Blue Coats to slaughter their people.

On the fourth day of the council the white peace men sat on their canvas chairs, flanked by their Blue Coats. One by one the Sioux chiefs came to sit cross-legged before them. A cloud of dust appeared on the hillside. Crazy Horse with the zigzag lightning mark on his cheek, the hawk on the side of his head and the eagle feather sticking up in his black hair rode slowly down the hill followed by a line of warriors. These were the ones who had said they would kill the first Sioux who spoke up for selling their beloved *Pa Sapa*.

Slowly they formed a double circle riding around and around the council meeting, while no word was uttered.

This went on endlessly it seemed. The Indian chiefs made a small knot and smoked and whispered to one another, but no one rose to speak. The white men teetered on their chairs nervously. The air of tension over the place increased.

Suddenly there was a shout as a young warrior broke through the circle of people, his rifle upraised.

"I have come to kill!" he cried, his eyes wild. "To kill the whites who would steal our land."

Crazy Horse jerked his horse in front of the warrior and put up his hand. "Stop!" he cried, and the power that came from him was strong. "Would you spoil everything we have planned? Go back to your lodge until you can act with the wisdom of a true Lakota."

For a long moment his glance bored into that of the young man; then the warrior turned his horse and rode through the circle. Slowly other warriors followed him. The chiefs got to their feet and left the meeting one by one

and the crowd melted away leaving the white peace men sitting pale-faced and large-eyed.

As Crazy Horse rode toward his lodge he knew that he had never been closer to death than he had that day. But his medicine was good. And he knew, too, that never had he been so great among the Lakotas. Now he was their leader indeed even though he had been unshirted by the Big Bellies who would follow the white man's way. But that did not matter now. He was strong among his people. He had kept them from trouble — for this one day, at least. But would his power be great enough to keep them from the trouble which was sure to follow?

TROUBLE!

WITH THE BREAKING UP of the council the Hunkpapa
Sioux under Sitting Bull moved back into the Black Hills
which still belonged to the Lakotas, and Crazy Horse, with
the Oglalas, moved north to the Powder River country.
Soon after he made his camp, small bands of people who
had stolen away from the reservations came to join him on
the Tongue River.

It was the winter the white men called 1875. Snow fell
early and with it came cold that chilled the bones. Crazy
Horse's people scattered in order to find better feed for the
ponies and better hunting, but there was gnawing hunger
in the camps as there had been every snow since the buffalo
had grown scarce.

The thaw of the Moon of Frost in the Lodge did not
come this year at its usual time and the Oglalas huddled in

their tents trying to conserve their energy while they waited for spring. Never, even in the memory of the oldest man among them, had anyone known such a cold winter.

Messengers came from the soldier fort saying that all Sioux must come to the reservation by the end of January or they would be considered hostiles and a large body of soldiers would move against them.

Crazy Horse rode over to the Hunkpapa village to talk over with Sitting Bull this latest, ridiculous demand of the white chiefs. Everyone knew that even lone men on horseback could not get to the reservation in this sort of weather by the time the white chief had set. To transport women and children and belongings that far in that length of time was completely impossible.

Sitting Bull chuckled as he told of the note he had sent back. "Come and get me," he had a half-breed in his camp write. "You won't need any guides. You can find me easily. I won't run away."

But Crazy Horse did not respond to his friend's wry humor. His face was serious.

"In the spring there will be trouble," he said.

Sitting Bull shrewdly had been collecting as many guns as he could get his hands on. His people had gone up into Canada and traded with the Slota Indians for firearms. Now he generously divided his supply with Crazy Horse's people. Fortunate that he did, for the troops did not wait for spring. Hoping to catch the Indians while their ponies were still weak, they pushed forward in the middle of March. They were led by Frank Grouard, a half-breed Hawaiian, who had been a pony express rider once and who had been captured by Sitting Bull's people. The chief had adopted him as his son and this half-breed who was called the Grab-

ber, lived among the Sioux for years. For a time after some
trouble with Sitting Bull he had lived with He Dog in
Crazy Horse's camp.

It was this camp of Crazy Horse's upon which the soldiers
stumbled at dawn before the Sioux were awake. One battalion was sent to take the pony herd; a second was ordered
to attack the village, while the third rode behind the camp
to cut off escape should any attempt be made.

At the first shot the Indians came pouring from their
tepees in a panic, many of them naked, running for the
hills. It looked like the usual easy victory for the soldiers
when an Indian village was taken by surprise in the early
morning.

"*Hoka hey! Hoka hey!*" Crazy Horse's strong voice rang
through the camp. "They have come. The Blue Coat
enemies who will wipe us out. Be brave! My men, protect
our village!"

Crazy Horse had trained his warriors well. As always
when confronted by an emergency, strength seemed to
emanate from him to his fighters. With satisfaction he saw
their panic give way to level thinking. The Oglalas sta-
tioned themselves behind the rocks lining the hills and
made every bullet, every arrow count. Most of their ponies
had been taken and they were afoot, but the formation of
the hilly ground was in their favor.

Crazy Horse strode between the lines of soldiers and his
own men. Bullets rained about him but without harming
him. *Hau!* His medicine was good this day. His coolness
and bravery inspired his warriors.

The soldiers were setting fire to the tepees. It made
Crazy Horse wince every time he heard one of the precious
powder kegs explode in the tepees. But the soldiers were

having a poor time of it, being fired upon from every side by warriors whose aim was determined and true.

Suddenly the soldiers began retreating, leaving their dead and several wounded behind.

"*Hoka hey! Hoka hey!*" Crazy Horse cried. "Don't let them get away."

The warriors raced after the retreating soldiers, but only a few of them had ponies, and it was impossible to overtake the Blue Coats on their horses. That night Crazy Horse led his braves in a raid in which they recovered a large number of their ponies which had been taken that morning.

That day was celebrated by the best victory dance that had been held for many moons.

With new dangers threatening, the camps were moved closer together again. Most of the lodges had been destroyed and Crazy Horse's people were forced to move in with friends until poles could be cut for new tepees. Everyone was busy. New arrows were made, bows put in shape, war clothing made ready, for no one doubted that the soldiers would come marching and shooting again.

Crazy Horse sent runners north to barter for more guns and ammunition from the Slotas, south to spy on the soldiers and their movements. They must not catch him off guard again.

A message came that another soldier chief named Crook was planning to march against his people. Crazy Horse sent word to the white chief that the Blue Coats must not cross the Tongue River. Crook straightway set out with twelve hundred experienced men. Crazy Horse met them with a handful of braves on the opposite bank of the Tongue and fired on the Blue Coats from a distance, injuring two. Then the Crazy Horse band raced off.

Crook camped on the Tongue for four days while each day Crazy Horse and his men rode up and down on the other side of the river, daring him to cross. In the middle of June Frank Grouard came up to aid Crook with three hundred Crow and Shoshone scouts.

That bright day in June from a hillside lookout point Crazy Horse watched that strong force splash across the Tongue River. They followed the trail leading into a wide valley surrounded by high bluffs. The Crow scouts rode out ahead, eager to rout out their deadly enemies, the Sioux. On the soldiers galloped, panting for revenge.

Four of the Crows rode to the top of the hill to scout. Sioux rifles crackled. What they saw sent the Crows galloping down the hill pell-mell, shouting, "Sioux! Heap many Sioux!"

The cry was no sooner out of their mouths than the hillside sprouted painted Sioux warriors. At first the soldiers were panicked by the suddenness of the onrush. They were not used to Indians who fought like white men. Soon Crook got his troops under control and sent out a three-pronged attack under command of Mills. Crazy Horse was alarmed to see Mills's battalion force one band of Sioux into temporary retreat, but as the soldiers advanced up the hill they found the Indians increasing in number.

The fight had been raging fiercely for two hours when Crazy Horse saw a weakness in the enemy position and sent a band of picked warriors charging like a pack of yelling fiends into the enemy flank.

Never had the soldiers met such furious fighting, where the enemy charged head on with such determination — and such surprising skill.

The troops started to retreat down the valley with the

yelling Sioux galloping after them, Crazy Horse at their head, like the darting tongue of a rattlesnake.

Meantime, a second battalion under Mills was hurrying down a gulch called Death Canyon where Crazy Horse's camp was located. While the other troops were engaged in fighting the Sioux along the hillsides, Mills expected to surprise the unprotected camp. Crazy Horse let out a yell of triumph. Things were going just as he had planned. Then his shouts died in his throat as he saw a messenger galloping up the canyon, obviously with orders, for immediately Mills's force retreated, without attacking the camp. They were not marching into his trap!

Crazy Horse chased Crook back across the Tongue River, then went to his village to watch the Sioux celebrate the victory. As his people danced, he sat hunched over, with his chin resting on his palms, watching. It had been a smashing victory. His people were right in celebrating. Yet he was not satisfied. He had planned a neat ambush of the battalion riding up Death Canyon. Had they gone only a little farther, they would have turned a corner — and that would have been the finish. They would have been surrounded and cut off. Nevertheless he could not grumble over the way the fighting had gone. No one had spoiled the plan by dashing out for coups. His warriors at last had learned to follow orders, to fight as a unit, for the good of all the people instead of for individual honors. With his warriors fighting so well, it might be that his people could keep their own lands after all. Perhaps the Blue Coats had learned their lesson and would leave them alone after today.

"MANY SOLDIERS FALLING INTO CAMP" 21

AT A GREAT MEETING of the tribes, Sitting Bull had been made chief of all the Lakotas. In Crazy Horse's opinion it was a good choice. The old Hunkpapa was a medicine man rather than a warrior, with the power to control the weather and to see into the future. His medicine was good. He had kept his people together all through the troubled times and it was his policy to stay far away from the whites, not accepting their presents and not fighting them. So his Hunkpapa Sioux band had not been divided as had the Oglalas, Miniconjous and Cheyennes and others by having some in favor of going to the reservations and some holding out for the old way of living.

Crazy Horse agreed with Sitting Bull that it was best for his people to stay as far from the white man as they could in order to avoid trouble, but that if they must fight in order to hold what was their own, they must be ready to do so; they should not submit to being driven from their own hunting grounds.

It was natural that Crazy Horse should camp with his band of Oglalas near the Hunkpapa village.

The Cheyennes and Miniconjou Sioux also pitched their tepees close to the stronger camps. Crazy Horse was glad to see the painted tepees stretch far up the creek beds. Never had there been such a gathering of Plains Indians. Having so many grouped together, however, made it difficult to keep the camps supplied with meat. It was necessary to send hunters out every day to look for game and every two or three sleeps the villages must be moved to new hunting grounds and fresh grass.

Hoye! What a good sight to see such a great band moving in the old way with the Big Bellies riding ahead, the scouts fanning out in all directions, the women and girls dressed in their prettiest garments, the boys whooping and galloping their horses up and down the line in a true boy show-off way. The Cheyennes traveled ahead followed by the Oglalas, because these two bands were the most experienced in fighting the soldiers. Then came the Miniconjous, with the Hunkpapas in the rear.

The grass was late this spring and the ponies not strong, so the progress was slow as the great band trailed northward. On a tributary of the Powder River the Sans Arcs Sioux joined the band, making five camps. With so many villages close together there was much visiting back and forth, with many ceremonial and social dances. This way of living was better, Crazy Horse thought with satisfaction, than being cooped up on the reservations under the rule of the white men. There was still plenty of game if the young men spent their time hunting for it instead of fighting.

What if they did have to keep constantly on the move? Wasn't that the Plains Indians' way of life?

When the tribes made camp in a pleasant valley where a tributary flowed into the Powder River, the Blackfeet came down from the north to join them. The meeting of the tribes was like numerous streams flowing together, forming a big river.

One day he saw the women erecting an arbor of boughs large enough to shelter many people. Evidently a council of the Oglalas was about to be held. But why hadn't he been told of it? Since he had come to such prominence among the Sioux, he was always invited to every council of importance. He saw several of the old men leaders gathered in a knot talking before the lodge of White Eagle. As he approached they stopped talking and foolish, half-guilty expressions passed over their faces. Sudden resentment flared up in Crazy Horse. They had been talking about him — he was sure of that. Even He Dog had avoided him lately, wearing a secretive, mysterious air.

The next afternoon he saw the chiefs of all the tribes and the old men counselors walk slowly toward the arbor and all of the people gather around. No one came to bid him go to the arbor. Hurt struggled with anger in his heart.

He sat before his tepee working on a bow, pretending not to notice nor to care what was going on. Finally He Dog came up and said, "Why aren't you at the council?"

"Why was I not asked?" Crazy Horse asked him bluntly.

"Were you not asked?" said He Dog as though it were a matter of not much consequence. "They probably forgot about you."

It was on the point of Crazy Horse's tongue to blurt out, "Have I become of so little importance among my people that they forget me in councils? I, who but a few sleeps ago

was called the greatest warrior the Lakotas ever had!" But he held the words back.

"I am busy," he said briefly. "The council does not need me."

Crazy Horse sat stony-faced. Pride held him from letting his friend know the bitterness and hurt that was gnawing his heart.

"A matter having to do with the good of the people is being discussed," He Dog said. "I have been sent to get you."

Crazy Horse's eyes widened. Was he to be reprimanded before the council? The hurt over the neglect he had suffered, which had been festering within his mind, nearly found outlet in quick, angry words, but he held them back and got slowly to his feet.

The arbor was crowded. He Dog tried to push Crazy Horse forward, but he, feeling many eyes upon him, held back and sat close to the entrance. He would not endure having those who were unfriendly over him gloat over his discomfiture any longer than possible.

Sitting Bull was speaking, saying solemnly, "The Lakotas have been through trying times. You know that I have always counseled my band to stay away from the white men and not go out looking for trouble. It is my opinion that this advice is good for all the Plains Indians."

He sat down and White Eagle arose and announced that a new chief of the Oglalas was to be chosen. "This is a serious matter," he said. "In his hands we will place the welfare of the people. No man should be chosen who has not shown himself strong and worthy of such great trust. After much council among all of the head men we have at last decided upon the one worthy to receive this honor."

Crazy Horse looked about the crowd curiously, wondering who had been chosen. While he was still wondering he felt himself being seized by the arms, raised to his feet and hustled to the center. Bull Elk and White Eagle lighted the long pipe, offered it to the four directions and then handed it to Crazy Horse.

He gasped with surprise and stared at them uncomprehendingly for a long moment.

"It is for you," White Eagle told him. "You are the

chosen one. In your hands we place the welfare of the Oglalas."

Crazy Horse put forth a hand that trembled and took the pipe and put it to his mouth. As he smoked, the old men placed over his shoulders a cape made from the skin of a spotted calf. It was as if they were placing a mantle of responsibility upon his back.

Never had Crazy Horse been so surprised and so moved by any happening. Great warriors were not always made chiefs and he knew that there were many among his tribesmen who were envious and who had worked to keep him from getting too big among the Lakotas. But now this greatest honor of all was put into his hands. He was pleased, humble and a trifle frightened.

After the ceremony he went out and gave away all of his horses but one, and his finest garments and riding equipment, robes and bows and arrows, as was the Sioux custom. The people followed him as he distributed his goods to needy persons, who sang songs of praise for his greatness and generosity.

Later he went alone to the hills to give thanks to the Great Holy Mystery, and to pray for guidance and wisdom in leading his people. As he stood on the hilltop he remembered his boyhood dreams of greatness. His dreams had come true and a great elation filled his soul — yet he was troubled, too, for this greatness had not been attained without cost. His leadership had lost him friends, and the weight of new responsibility seemed very heavy.

"Guidance *Wakan Tanka!* More guidance," he prayed. "Give me strength and wisdom to lead my people to safety and to peace."

He stretched out his arms and sent his spirit forth to join the Holy Mystery — but there was no feeling of union. A chill entered his heart as the sun went under a cloud. His weary arms finally dropped to his sides.

Slowly he walked back to the village. Was the *Wakan Tanka* displeased with him? His feet felt heavy as stones as he walked between the rows of tepees and a weight of depression smothered his soul.

The camps moved west from the Powder River, gathering more bands as they traveled. It seemed that all the wandering Indians of the plains had heard of the greatness of Sitting Bull, the medicine man, and of Crazy Horse, the Oglala warrior, and sought protection under them. Some Sans Arcs had joined them as well as some No Clothes people who had been fleeing from the whites for many moons. They were so called because they had almost nothing to wear and no horses or lodges, and the travois bearing their few pitiful belongings were pulled by dogs.

Word came to the big camp that the white chief called Yellow Hair was roaming the country. The Cheyennes set up the keening sound when they heard this news, in memory of their southern friends who had been wiped out by this terrible fighting man.

Some of the young warriors wanted to ride out and chase Yellow Hair from their country, but Crazy Horse forbade it — he counseled not to fight until the Blue Coats attacked.

As he looked out over the great circle of tepees — at the ponies thick as grasshoppers on the hills he felt sure when the soldiers saw them they would not attack such great numbers as theirs. *Hau!* It was wise to give themselves strength by banding together this way. If they had done it long ago there would have been no soldier trouble.

They moved on up the Rosebud to the valley of the Little Big Horn — the greasy grass country.

"*Was-te!* It is good!" Crazy Horse said to He Dog as he

looked over the big encampment. "Now we are out of the white man's country. He can live there and we can live here."

The Hunkpapas held their great Medicine Dance near

their sacred Deer Medicine rocks. All of the other bands came to look on, although they did not participate. To prove how strong was his medicine Sitting Bull took the torture test in which he allowed fifty pieces of flesh to be cut from each arm, singing while the cutting was being done, and facing the sun all day, without food or water, until he went into a trance as the sun fell over the edge of the world.

When he came back from the blackness he held out both hands. "In my medicine dream I saw many soldiers," he said. "Many soldiers falling into camp upside down."

After the Hunkpapa Medicine Dance there was a big social celebration in which all the camps took part, going from village to village, with much laughter, the beating of drums and singing. The merry-making lasted until the darkness grew thin, and most of the weary people stumbled off to their sleeping robes.

It was the middle of the Moon When the Animals Are Fat, and as the day woke the sun shone down upon a camp still drowsy from the celebration. Some children splashed in the river trying to cool themselves, but few of the older people were fully awake when a cry rang through the villages. "A-h-h-h! Soldiers coming. Many soldiers on the way!"

It was like a cannon booming through the summer stillness. Boys raced to drive in the ponies for the warriors. The fighters themselves hurried to daub on war paint. Crazy Horse had slept in the Cheyenne camp. He ran all the way to his lodge to fasten the red hawk on the side of his head, to make the zigzag lightning streak on his face and to get out his bag of dust from a gopher hole to throw over his war horse for protection, and to don his spotted cape.

Her-Black-Robe, in spite of being weak from the coughing sickness, had the bridle on his pony by the time he was
ready. He galloped toward the Hunkpapa village where
already puffs of smoke from the soldier guns were dotting
the hillside.

Screaming women grabbed up small children and ran
toward the hills. Dogs yapped. Young men leaped upon
the horses the boys drove into camp. Slapping their mouths
with their hands to make the war cry they raced forward
to meet the soldiers.

"Be calm!" Crazy Horse shouted. "Be brave. This is a
good day to die."

He knew that this day his medicine was good. Power
surged through his veins. He leaned forward on his spotted
horse.

"*Hoka-hey!*" he shouted the cry to charge. His voice was
big and carried back to the young men following him.
Although this was Sitting Bull's camp that was being
attacked, the Oglalas and Cheyennes joined the Hunkpapas
in defense.

Seeing such a strong force before them, the soldiers dismounted to fight. The Indians dismounted, too. Crazy
Horse noted with satisfaction that it was a good fight. Many
brave deeds were being done by his men. They were fighting together. The soldier chief, Reno, appeared to be in
a panic. His men did not seem to understand what he
wanted them to do. Then their guns jammed. They began
racing toward their horses, or back in the direction of a
hill with the yelling Indians close to their heels.

They splashed through the river, crowding each other.
The sight reminded Crazy Horse of a buffalo stampede.
There was only a narrow ravine leading up the hill where
the soldiers were trying to gain refuge. In their efforts to

escape the enemy, they clawed and pushed and tramped upon each other.

Before the Sioux had time to finish off the fleeing Blue Coats an Indian messenger galloped up.

Jerking his thumb wildly over his shoulder he gasped, Blue Coats! Many, many Blue Coats riding into other end of camp."

"*Hoye!*" Crazy Horse shouted. Then Sitting Bull's vision was coming true! Many soldiers falling into camp, as from the sky.

He put his eagle wing whistle to his lips and blew a shrill blast summoning his followers.

"Fight for all our people," he yelled. "This is a good day to die. Brave men follow me. Cowards to the rear."

He galloped to the head of his group of warriors leading the way to the end of the village. The camp, as he rode through it, was in a worse hubbub than at the first attack, with distracted mothers darting about looking for lost children and wailing children looking for their mothers; with dogs barking and horses rearing. When Crazy Horse rode past his tepee Her-Black-Robe ran and thrust the sacred lance of the Oglalas into his hand.

Was-te! This was good. Today the Oglalas had need of all of the sacred things so that their medicine would be strong. As Crazy Horse grasped the lance, he felt strength and power surge up in him.

He hated to see such panic in the village, but it was no wonder, with the warriors all drawn away to the far end of the camp and the women, old men and children left helpless.

Then he saw four Cheyenne braves ride out into the water to meet the soldiers riding down to ford the river. Only the four of them against the advancing Blue Coat

wave! They were his Cheyenne friends, Calf, Bobtail Horse, Roan Bear and Mad Wolf. There they sat like a wall, rifles ready, waiting. Never had Crazy Horse seen such a splendid thing.

"*Hoka-hey! Hoka-hey!*" he cried, urging his horse into the stream. "Hurry, my braves. We must not let our courageous Cheyenne friends be slain."

The horses of the Oglalas splashed into the river all around him.

The soldiers rode by fours. As they came closer to the ford, the Indians could recognize the leader.

"It is the hated one, Custer!" Bobtail Horse shouted. "Yellow Hair, who killed our people on the Washita!"

Bobtail's rifle spoke. Arrows flew. A Blue Coat fell from his horse. The soldiers drew back from the river and bunched along the ridge and dismounted. Then all became a confused muddle of yelling, of rifle shot, of dust hanging heavy over everything. The Lakota horses gained the other side of the river. Another band galloped up a dry gulch funneling into the hill where the yellow-haired chief had halted.

Crazy Horse looked into the face of the Oglala galloping beside him. At first he did not recognize the features although they were vaguely familiar. He peered again, amazed. It was the face of White Deerskin, a woman whose brother had been killed by Crook's soldiers.

He rose in the saddle, lifting the sacred lance high. "*Hay-ay! Hay-ay!*" he shouted. "Be brave, my men. A woman fights with us."

Through the dust Crazy Horse saw Custer's men swiftly mount their horses and race for the knob of a hill to the rear of the ridge. But another group of Indians galloped around to the rear of the ridge, cutting off this retreat.

Again most of the soldiers dismounted to shoot from the knee, or to use the fallen horses as barricades. The yelling Indians swirled around the ridge. Some were on horseback; many more were creeping from bush to bush up the gulches, along the hillsides. Here arrows were an advantage because the warriors could fire them in a high arc. The arrows stuck into the horses and sent them plunging, knocking down the soldiers in their way. The screaming horses, the sharp cracks of rifle fire, the fiendish yells of the Indians, the cries of dying men, the smell of smoke, dust and blood burned an impression on Crazy Horse which he would never forget.

The Indians in the gullies crept nearer and nearer to the soldier group. Those on horseback swirled and eddied about the Blue Coats, darting in to fire, dashing out again to be replaced by still others. In the confusion, Sioux sometimes slew Sioux, but the band of gallant Blue Coats on the hillside was getting smaller and smaller and at last the firing ceased altogether. The Indians swooped upon the slain enemies to count coup and to loot and to mutilate the bodies so that these Blue Coats would not be able to fight them when they all reached the Happy Hunting Ground.

Crazy Horse could scarcely believe his eyes when he stared at the scene. Every Blue Coat dead. And in such a short time of fighting. The sun was just past the middle. His eyes ran quickly over the battlefield. Over two hundred soldiers by the white man's way of counting, he guessed.

There had been a short time of silence after the firing ceased — an eerie contrast to the cracking and booming and yelling of a short time before. But now there was noise and confusion again — savage yells as the warriors and women slashed the bodies. Crazy Horse saw several Cheyennes

standing guard over one of the slain ones. He rode over
to see who it was. Two Moons stepped aside so that he
could look at the body — that of a white soldier in a buckskin shirt.

"Why do you not take his scalp — strip him?" Crazy
Horse asked.

"It is the big chief — Yellow Hair," Two Moons replied.
"He was our enemy. We hated him. But he was too brave
to scalp. He must not be stripped or harmed. I myself
counted third coup upon him."

Crazy Horse turned away, riding over the battleground.
The dust was lifting now. He looked down at the white,
still faces. These men had fought bravely. But why had
they come killing? Their chief, Custer, had been crazily
reckless — had certainly underestimated the strength of the
combined forces of the Indians.

After the frenzied fighting Crazy Horse experienced a
deadening depression. He had never been so weary. The
other Indians, too, rode around looking bewildered by their
quick triumph. Now the bodies lay naked beneath the hot
sun, their white skin looking bleached and unhealthy.

The warriors urged their weary, lathered horses toward
the hill where the soldiers of the earlier battle still huddled
in terror. Crazy Horse watched them go. His heart was
now cold for battle. He did not wish his men to fight again.
They must not use up all of their powder. They had got
many new guns from the slain soldiers, but not much ammunition.

He rode slowly back to camp thinking of the brave things
he had seen this day — of the way his men fought now for
the safety of the people rather than for personal glory. This
was the way he had taught them to fight; his long struggle
had been worth while.

NO PLACE TO STAY

■■■■■■■ **22**

CRAZY HORSE and his people knew that they must have scored the greatest victory of all time over the whites, yet he withdrew to his tepee having no heart to enter into the victory dance. The Indians had lost many of their number and when the keening that night became so loud that Crazy Horse could not sleep, he arose and went to stand alone on a hillside. The campfires flared high. The Indians were breaking camp, for no one wanted to linger so close to a battlefield where the dead still lay above the ground white and ghostly. The scaffolds beside the river where the Indians placed their dead were many and the tepees of those who had been slain were being burned.

Thinking over the happenings of the day — the good fighting, the many brave deeds done, the smashing victory over the soldiers, Crazy Horse wondered why his heart was

like a stone with no joy in it. He tried to make himself believe that now the soldiers, having learned the strength of
the Indians, would leave them alone to live as they pleased.
But he could not make his mind accept this conclusion.
The whites were vengeful. They would not allow the death
of their brave Custer and his entire command to go un-
punished. What would be the final outcome?

The following day more troops came riding in a cloud of
dust. But there was no battle. They looked over the battleground of the day before, rescued Reno, buried the bodies,
and went away.

Crazy Horse and Sitting Bull discussed what was best to
do now. Surely the soldiers would come again. It was best
to flee, they decided.

"In smaller bands we can move faster," said Crazy Horse.
"We will be harder to find. We have used up most of our
ammunition."

Sitting Bull agreed. So the Indians scattered to the four
winds. General Miles and his troops drove Sitting Bull
clear to Canada. Crazy Horse hid out in the Powder River
country. Many of the Cheyennes went onto the reservation
and some of the Oglalas joined Red Cloud on the reservation which bore his name. Crazy Horse tried to hold his
people together. He knew that his own bitterness toward
the whites would never diminish and that only misery
would come to his people if they were ever forced to bow
down to the whites. To him, life on a reservation would
be worse than death.

"Better to die fighting than to rot away — or starve to
death on an agency," he told his people over and over again
as times grew more difficult for them. "Only the woman-
hearted give up to go on the reservations — to be penned
up like the white men's cows. It is worse than ever now

that the agencies have been put under control of the Blue Coats."

Soon came word from the Red Cloud agency that bound the people of Crazy Horse more closely to him. The fall meat was being made when a news walker told that the holy land of the Sioux, the Black Hills, was sold.

Crazy Horse leaped to his feet, his eyes ablaze when the word was brought to his tepee. "That cannot be true!" he cried. "The Great Father promised that the land was ours so long as the grass should grow and the waters flow, that the *Pa Sapa* would never be sold until three out of every four of our people should sign."

"The agency chiefs have signed," the messenger repeated. "The land is sold."

"Then," Crazy Horse shouted, "the white men gave our chiefs their fire water to make them lose their minds."

"No," the messenger said, "Red Cloud and Spotted Tail were shut in the soldier's stockade. Then the 'agreement' was read to them, saying that their land was being 'sold' in return for feeding their people and that they would be sent to the South Country."

"The South Country where the Cheyennes were sent to starve and die," Crazy Horse spat out the words. "The hot, dry country where nothing can grow. Nothing can live!" — The Dry Tortugas, Florida.

"They refused to sign at first," the messenger went on. "They told the agents that our people could not endure the South Country — that they wanted to remain on their own lands as had been promised them. Then the agents said that their children would not be fed until they signed the paper giving away part of the holy land. So rather than have their children starve, they put their hands to the pen."

Crazy Horse was so enraged that he could not talk. He

strode away to the hills to be alone. His heart was hot with hatred. Would there never be an end to the white man's treachery?

Winter came early and with a fury which matched Crazy Horse's own. But he could not settle his camp in some sheltered spot so that his people could stay snug in their tepees until spring. He must keep them ever on the move, playing hide and seek with the pursuing Blue Coats who were determined to drive them onto the reservation.

Bear Coat, General Miles, built a fort on the Yellowstone at the mouth of the Tongue River. Crazy Horse was not surprised. First the Black Hills were taken and now the Powder River country from which he had once driven the Blue Coats was being threatened again. Was there never to be any peace for their people, no matter how far away from the whites they stayed?

He moved his camp farther up the river and kept on moving it until his people were weary from so much traveling. It was not until the Moon of Popping Trees that Bear Coat caught up with him. Crazy Horse knew that he must at last take a stand. Now it had to be a fight to the finish. He could not keep running from the Blue Coats forever. He gathered his warriors together. It was early morning when they appeared on the ridges overlooking a valley below Wolf Mountain where the soldiers were encamped.

It looked like an easy surround to Crazy Horse as he led his yelling band on to charge. But suddenly the soldiers peeled back the canvas covering from two cannon. The great shells screeched through the cold air and exploded within the Sioux ranks. This was something the warriors feared beyond all else. They would have fled had it not been for Crazy Horse's firm leadership.

Although their ammunition was low, he held them together fighting hard until a blinding blizzard came up, when he was forced to withdraw.

He moved his camp again and managed to elude the soldiers for a few weeks longer. One day a half-breed messenger came into camp with a message ordering the Sioux to surrender. Crazy Horse thought of his people. Their condition was truly desperate. They were starving, suffering from frostbite and sickness and most of their horses dead. The Cheyennes who were with him gave up and accompanied the half-breed to the agency. Crazy Horse held out for several moons longer, but he could not bear the sight of his people's sufferings and at last he led his two thousand followers to Red Cloud's agency.

It was early in the Moon of Green Grass, when the Oglalas came in. Crazy Horse with the hawk on his head, was in the lead, flanked by his chiefs, He Dog, Little Big Man, Old Hawk, and Big Road. Their warriors marched behind them solemnly singing their brave heart song; the meaning now so ironic:

> Comrades, kinsmen,
>   Now have ye spoken thus,
> The earth is mine,
>   'Tis my domain.
> 'Tis said, and now I exert me!

The column was two miles long by the white man's measure. The soldiers were lined up in two rows making an aisle down which the conquered Oglalas must march. Behind the soldiers crowded the agency Indians. Crazy Horse froze his face so that no one could see his breaking heart as his moccasined feet carried him past the hated Blue

Coats to their chief. They had forced him to come in —
but never, never would he become an agency Indian, fawn-
ing on the white leaders for favors. Until his dying day
the bitterness would stay in his heart for these lying, thieving people who had destroyed the Lakota way of life.

The squaws set up the tepees on a barren spot where the
Blue Coats directed. Crazy Horse wanted to cry out when
he saw the soldiers going through everything the Oglalas
owned, seizing all guns, ammunition and war bonnets. He
had never been one for elaborate war garments, but when
the Blue Coats took away the red hawk he wore on his head
during battle and his bag of sacred war medicines with the
blue stone, he wanted to rush forward and seize his few
precious belongings.

When the soldiers took their horses, it was the supreme
insult. Now they were making walking Indians of a tribe
whose pride and strength had come with the ownership of
the horse — the symbol of their wealth and power. By this
means were they reduced to the lowliest type of red man.
By such humiliation did the agent hope to break their spirit
— especially that of their leader, Crazy Horse.

He wanted to die that day, but his heart kept on beating.
Before many moons he saw that there was a steady struggle
for power among the old-time leaders. Red Cloud, who had
been one of the first to come in to the agency and who had
gone to Washington to talk to the Great Father, had once
been Agency Chief. Now for some reason the power had
been taken from him and put into the hands of Spotted
Tail.

It made Crazy Horse turn away his face in shame to see
how Red Cloud and others now were all smiles and soft
ways toward the white chief in order to gain his favor —
and the power he could bestow. And it was great satisfac-

tion to Crazy Horse's battered pride to see that his people still followed his moccasin tracks, and that many others, also, were looking to him for leadership. But he knew, too, that the ones who sought hard for power were jealous of him and hated him because the people looked to him, without any power having been put into his hands by the agent.

In spite of the fact that he was still great among his own people, Crazy Horse was tasting the dregs of unhappiness. He detested the odor and the taste of the white men's whoa haws they had to eat and he longed for juicy buffalo meat. Her-Black-Robe boiled the slab of bacon they were given with their rations, but it was disgusting stuff that even the dogs would not eat. He put his hand into the sack of the white powder the white men called flour, took some out to sniff and taste. It had neither odor nor flavor. Her-Black-Robe dumped it on the ground and used the sack to make herself a dress.

The slow days dragged by with nothing to do. The agent had promised the Oglalas an old-time buffalo hunt. They talked about it and looked forward to it with childlike eagerness. But it was only another broken promise. Again hope died.

Crazy Horse sat before his canvas tepee thinking about death. He heard Her-Black-Robe cough. She was growing weaker from the coughing sickness and now did little but lie on her bed robes. She was growing very weak. He would like to take her to McGillicuddy, the white medicine man on Spotted Tail reservation — if he could borrow a horse and wagon.

He watched an eagle making wide circles overhead and envied its freedom. His head sank on his chest. Then it seemed he was standing on a high hill in the sacred *Pa Sapa*. The eagle was still soaring overhead. Then suddenly it folded its wings and dropped to the ground at his feet.

Amazed, Crazy Horse stared at it. The eagle was himself with an arrow through his heart.

He jerked upright and shook his head. The dream was so real that he was surprised to find himself still alive. What did it mean?

He went inside and looked down at Her-Black-Robe. She smiled at him weakly. "I would like to go to my own people," she said.

"*Hau!* I have been thinking of it," he said. "If I can get a wagon . . . "

He went outside frowning. Where could he get a wagon to take his wife to her own people at Spotted Tail. Slowly he walked to the office of the agent, hating to have to ask a favor of him, but the need was urgent.

"My wife has the coughing sickness," he told the agent. "I would like a wagon to take her to Spotted Tail. Her own people are there. And the white medicine man will help her."

"You will have to ask the President — the Great Father," the agent said curtly. "I have no power to grant such a request."

"I am not hunting for the Great Father," Crazy Horse said with dignity. "My Father is with me. No White Father stands between me and the Great Mystery."

He walked from the office. Somehow he must manage to get a wagon.

He Dog caught up with him. "Red Cloud and No Water," he said bitterly, "even the Grabber — the one who calls himself Grouard — he who lived as Sitting Bull's son and who sipped from the horn spoon in my lodge and in yours are telling the agent lies. They are saying that you are plotting to kill General Crook."

"They easily acquired the white man's habit of lying," Crazy Horse said, not much concerned.

"But they are trying to make trouble for you," He Dog cried.

Crazy Horse shrugged. "I am used to trouble," he said wearily. "We feed upon trouble and lies since we are under the white men."

A few days following this conversation the agent called Crazy Horse into the office and said that he had heard reports that the chief was plotting to kill General Crook.

Crazy Horse looked at him scornfully. "Only cowards are murderers," he said. "I am no coward."

He stalked from the room.

A few weeks later he was again called into the office. This time General Crook was there, as well as other Indians and soldiers.

"You have heard of the Nez Percé tribe being led by Chief Joseph," he said through the interpreter, Frank Grouard, the one the Indians called the Grabber. "Will you go out to fight them?"

"We are tired of fighting," Crazy Horse replied. "We came in for peace. But if the Great Father says we must go, we will go north and fight until there is not a Nez Percé left."

He noticed the crafty look which came over the Grabber's face as he jabbered in the white man's tongue. Crazy Horse detested this man who, by scouting for Crook against those in whose tepees he had dwelt, had turned traitor to those who had befriended him. He knew that the Grabber feared him.

Crazy Horse had thought that his words were simple and direct and he looked around the room in bewilderment when Crook and everyone else glared at him and then everyone started chattering excitedly.

It was not until later that he learned from a friend who

had a smattering of the white man's language the cause of the commotion.

"The Grabber twisted your words around," the friend told him. "He said the first part correctly; then he made your words out to be, 'We will go north and fight until not a white man is left.'"

"Phaugh!" Crazy Horse cried. "There is no such thing as truth in the Grabber. His heart is black and his tongue is crooked."

Crazy Horse could not waste time then discussing the Grabber's treachery. Jennie Thunderbird, one of the Oglalas who had come to the reservation early and so had won the privilege of keeping some horses, was traveling to the Spotted Tail reservation in a light wagon. She offered to take Crazy Horse and Her-Black-Robe.

He quickly bundled up her few clothes and thrust the hunting knife a friend had given him into his belt, then lifted her onto a pile of robes in the back of the wagon.

Before they reached Spotted Tail a squad of Indians — the "good" ones the agent had made soldiers, galloped up and surrounded the wagon.

"You are running away," War Dog cried. "We have come to arrest you."

Crazy Horse stood up in the wagon, the whip gripped in his hand. The eyes of those who had come after him dropped beneath his angry, scornful gaze. "I am Crazy Horse," he cried. "Do not touch me. I am not running away!"

His power over his people still held. There were twenty armed men in the squad come to arrest him, but they fell back at his command and quietly rode behind him to Spotted Tail reservation. There he put Her-Black-Robe in the care of Dr. McGillicuddy. Only then would he submit to being taken back to Red Cloud Reservation.

Crazy Horse looked at the twenty Indian soldiers. Several of his good friends were there, Touch-the-Clouds, High Bear, Horned Antelope and Little Big Man. He shrugged his shoulders as if it did not much matter what he did now.

"I will go," he said, "if I can ride a horse, as a chief should."

He was given a horse and the party set out, arriving at Red Cloud Reservation in late evening. There he was told that it was too late for a talk with Crook and the agent, but that he should go with the officer of the day, Captain Kennington, and that not a hair of his head would be harmed.

He followed the Captain. Two soldiers marched with him and his friends, Touch-the-Clouds, High Bear and Little Big Man were not far behind. The Captain stepped along briskly, then held open a door to a long building and motioned to Crazy Horse to enter.

Not until he was inside did the great chief realize what was being done to him. He saw the dungeon cells, the prisoners in irons, the small window with bars across. The white man's jail!

A roar like that of a trapped animal burst from his throat. Pushing everyone aside he dashed from the building, pulling his knife from his belt.

His arms were grabbed from behind. And by one of his own friends — Little Big Man. In the struggle Little Big Man's arm was cut to the bone.

"Kill him! Kill him!" Captain Kennington shouted. Then, while his arms were held, a guard thrust a bayonet into his side.

He grew limp in the hands of his prisoners. They released him and he sank to the ground.

They carried him to the office. The enraged Oglalas and

Brulés swirled about the place. Even his enemies shouted their anger over this thing that had been done to their great man.

His mother and father heard the news and hurried to the place. They were allowed to go in to stay beside him. Presently the seething crowd outside heard the voice of the elder Crazy Horse rise in the death song for his son. The moon passed beneath a cloud while they listened. Then the singing stopped and the keening commenced. They knew that Crazy Horse had gone to the great Beyond.

It was as well that Crazy Horse had gone. He died as he had wanted to — fighting. It was better so than if he had lived to see the sad thing that was to be the fate of his people. They were being readied to move to the South Country — that hated, burned up land to which any red-blooded Sioux much preferred death.

His mother and father were allowed to wrap his body in the trappings of a warrior and to place it on a scaffold. Later the officials demanded that they take the body down for they were planning to bury it in the reservation burial grounds.

"He would not like to be put beneath the ground here on this hated place," his father protested.

"That is the way it must be," the official told him. "To-morrow a grave will be dug."

The old people, however, made a travois and in the night took the body away into the hills. When they returned neither threats nor bribes could make them tell what they had done with their son's body.

"We gave Crazy Horse back to the land of his people," was all that they would say.

THE END

CRAZY HORSE 1840(?)–1877

1840–44? Date uncertain. Born on Republican River. He is named Has-ka, the light-skinned one.

1845: First caravan of settlers crosses the plains.

1849: During time of famine in camp he invites old men and women in to feast on two antelopes his father killed.

The gold rush.

Fort Laramie bought as a military post.

1851: Father gives him own pony which he must break himself.

Great Fort Laramie Treaty Council, to establish roads and military posts and to bring peace to Plains tribes in return for annuities.

1852: Saves brother from grizzly bear attack.

1853: Has-ka's first buffalo hunt. Rides buffalo calf.

1854: Has-ka goes on wild horse hunt. Rides splendid animal and earns his name, Crazy Horse.

Young Crazy Horse witnesses the Grattan Massacre — the first massacre on the Plains.

1855: The Vision Quest. After purification rites, Crazy Horse goes alone to a hilltop to fast for three days and to pray for a vision. A hawk brings him a message from the Great Mystery. Because the hawk has proved himself his brother, Crazy Horse will wear the head of a hawk on the side of his own head at all ceremonies.

Battle of Blue Water, September 3.

1857: Big Sioux Council near Bear Butte.

Horse stealing expedition against Crows. Crazy Horse organizes it and earns leadership. Takes part in the Sundance.

1859: The Pony Express.

1860: Joins a war party against the Gros Ventres. Distinguishes himself by saving the life of the great warrior, High Backbone (Hump). The two become inseparable companions.

1861: Meets with council of Teton Sioux to decide upon policy toward white men. Crazy Horse speaks up for strong resistance.

1861: Civil War draws soldiers from frontier posts. Telegraph to California completed.

1863: Bozeman Trail through Sioux Powder River country established. Crazy Horse has by this time proved himself as a warrior leader. The Indians had never had a disciplined form of attack; they always fought for individual honors. Now Crazy Horse starts drilling them in teamwork fighting.

1864: The Sand Creek Massacre led by Chivington, in Colorado, Nov. 29. This led to the uniting of the Plains tribes and was the cause of the outbreak of the Plains Indian warfare.

Crazy Horse is made a chief.

1865: Platte River Fight.

Powder River Expedition under Connor.

Harney-Sanborn Treaty.

1866: Forts Reno and Phil Kearny built on the Bozeman Trail, through the country that had been promised to the Sioux.

Crazy Horse vows unceasing warfare upon the whites.

Fort Kearny is held under constant siege.

Fetterman Massacre, December 21.

1867: Union Pacific Railway pushes through Sioux country.

Wagon Box Fight, near Fort Phil Kearny, Aug. 2.

1868: Attack on old Horsecreek Station by Crazy Horse. March 19.

Signing of Treaty of 1868, promising the Sioux all of the Black Hills and the Powder River Country.

1870: Crazy Horse with other Sioux chiefs taken to Washington to meet with the Great White Father.

1872: Baker Fight.

1873: Custer Fight, Aug. 14, 1872.

1874: Black Hills Expedition under Custer.

1875: Jenney Expedition into Black Hills.

Opening of the "Thieves Road."

Lone Tree Council for sale of Black Hills.

1876: Reynold's fight, March 17.

Rosebud Battle, June 17.

Custer "Massacre," June 25.

Sibley Scouts attacked, July 17.

Miles' fight with Sitting Bull, Oct. 21.

Dull Knife Fight, Nov. 25.

Sioux chiefs killed at Fort Keogh, December.

1877: Miles strikes Crazy Horse, Jan. 8.

Crazy Horse surrenders, May 6.

Railroad Strike, summer.

Nez Percé outbreak, summer.

Crazy Horse tries to take his wife, dying of the white man's coughing sickness, to her people. The white men accuse him of trying to run away and use this as an excuse to kill him. Only Death was able to break Crazy Horse's power over his people.

■■■■■■■■ BIBLIOGRAPHY ■■■■■■■■

Annals of Wyoming, Sitting Bull Deals With a Rebel. Wyoming State Historical Society, October, 1929.

Bent, George to George Hyde, *Bent Letters*. State Historical Society of Colorado, 1905.

Boyd, James, *Indian Wars*. Philadelphia: Publishers' Union, 1891.

Brady, Cyrus Townsend, *Indian Fights and Fighters*. Garden City, New York: Doubleday, Page, 1904.

Britt, Albert, *Great Indian Chiefs*. New York: Whittlesey House, 1938.

Bulletin 61, Bureau of American Ethnology, *Teton Sioux Music*. Washington, D.C.

Bureau of American Ethnology Bulletin, Part 2.

Burt, Struthers, *Powder River*. New York: Farrar and Rinehart, 1939.

Chief Luther Standing Bear, *My People the Sioux*. Boston: Houghton Mifflin Company, 1928.

Chittenden, Hiram M., and Alfred T. Richardson, eds., *Life, Letters and Travels of Father Pierre Jean De Smet, S.J. Among the North American Indians*. New York: Harper and Brothers, 1905.

Chittenden, Hiram M., *The American Fur Trade of the Far West*. New York: Press of the Pioneers, 1935.

Coutant, C. G., *The History of Wyoming*. Laramie, Wyoming: Chaplin, Spafford and Mathison, 1899.

Crozier, Major L. E. F., *Sitting Bull's Account of Custer's Last Fight*. Canadian Historical Journal, 1835.

Curtis, Natalie, *The Indian Book*. New York: Harper and Brothers, 1907.

DeBarthe, F., *The Life and Adventures of Frank Grouard*. St. Joseph, Missouri: Combe Publishing Company, 1894.

DeLand, Charles E., *The Sioux Wars*. Pierre, South Dakota: in South Dakota Historical Collections, Vol. XV, Department of History.

Dorsey, James Owen, *Siouan Indian Religion and Mythology.* Washington, D.C.: U.S. Bureau of Ethnology, 11th Annual Report, 1889–90.

Eastman, Charles A., *Indian Boyhood.* Boston: Little Brown and Company, 1902.

Embree, Edwin R., *Indians of America.* Boston: Houghton Mifflin Company, 1939.

Garst, Shannon, *Sitting Bull: Champion of the Sioux.* New York: Julian Messner, Inc., 1946.

Garst, Shannon, *Custer: Fighter of the Plains.* New York: Julian Messner, Inc., 1942.

Garst, Shannon, *When the West Was Young.* Douglas, Wyoming: Enterprise Company, 1942.

Garst, Shannon, *Kit Carson: Trail Blazer and Scout.* New York: Julian Messner, Inc., 1942.

Garst, Shannon, *Buffalo Bill: Greatest of the Scouts.* New York: Julian Messner, Inc., 1948.

Godfrey, Gen. E. S., *Custer's Last Battle.* Century Magazine, Jan., 1892.

Hafen, LeRoy, Ph.D., Litt.D., and Francis Marion Young, A.B., *Fort Laramie and the Pageant of the West,* 2 vols. Glendale, California: The Arthur H. Clark Company, 1938.

Hebard, Grace Raymond, *The Pathbreakers from River to Ocean.* Chicago: Lakeside Press, 1913.

Hunt, Frazier, and Robert, *I Fought With Custer, The Story of Sergeant Windolph, Last Survivor of the Battle of the Little Big Horn,* as told to Frazier and Robert Hunt. New York: Scribner's, 1947.

Hyde, George E., *Red Cloud's Folk: A History of the Oglala Sioux Indians.* Norman, Oklahoma: University of Oklahoma Press, 1937.

Johnson, Willis Fletcher, *Life of Sitting Bull.* Edgewood, South Dakota: Edgewood Publishing Company, 1891.

Marquis, Thomas B., *A Warrior Who Fought Custer.* Minneapolis, Minnesota: Midwest Publishing Company, 1931.

McLaughlin, James M., *My Friend the Indian.* Boston: Houghton Mifflin Company, 1930.

Miles, Gen. Nelson A., *Personal Recollections of.* Chicago: Werner Company, 1897.

Moorehead, Warren K., *The American Indian in the United States.* Andover, Maine: Andover Press, 1914.

Sabin, Edwin L., *Kit Carson Days.* New York: Press of the Pioneers, 1935.

Sabin, Edwin L., *Boy's Book of Indian Warriors.* Philadelphia: George W. Jacobs Company, 1918.

Sandoz, Mari, *Crazy Horse.* New York: Alfred A. Knopf, 1942.

Shield, Col. G. O., *The Blanket Indian of the Northwest.* New York: Vichten Waring, 1921.

South Dakota Historical Collections, *Some Sidelights on the Character of Sitting Bull,* Doane Robinson, Vol. 5. Pierre, South Dakota: State Publishing Company, 1910.

Spring, Agnes, *Caspar Collins.* New York: Columbia University Press, 1927.

Superintendent of Indian Affairs, *Letter Book.* Topeka, Kansas: Among the manuscripts of the Kansas Historical Society.

Vestal, Stanley, *Sitting Bull.* Boston: Houghton Mifflin Company, 1932.

Walsh, Richard J., *The Making of Buffalo Bill.* New York: A. L. Burt, 1928.

Wellman, Paul E., *Death on the Prairie.* New York: The Macmillan Company, 1934.

Wissler, Clark, Curator of Anthropology, *North American Indians.* Lancaster, Pennsylvania: Lancaster Press, 1934.

Wissler, Clark, *Indians of the United States.* New York: Doubleday, Doran, 1940.